D0090227

OLD FAITHFUL

OLD FAITHFUL

18 Writers Present
Their Favorite Writing Assignments

Edited by Christopher Edgar & Ron Padgett

Teachers & Writers Collaborative
New York, N.Y.

Old Faithful: 18 Writers Present Their Favorite Writing Assignments

Acknowledgments
Paul Beatty's "Gription" reprinted by permission of the author from his *Big Bank Take Little Bank*, © 1991. Joy Harjo's "Eagle Poem" and "Song for the Deer and Myself to Return On" from *In Mad Love and War* © 1990 by Joy Harjo, Wesleyan University Press reprinted by permission of University Press of New England. Columbia University Press for Burton Watson's translation of Li Po's "Spring Night in Lo-Yang" in *Chinese Lyricism*, copyright © 1971 by Columbia University Press. Ramson Lomatewama's "An Evening at Windy Point for Christopher Jay" reprinted by permission of the author from his *Ascending the Reed*. Barry Lane's "Red Light 10 A.M. June 17, 1991" reprinted by permission of the author. Victor Hernández Cruz's "Theory of Why Night Comes" from *Red Beans* reprinted by permission of Coffee House Press, © 1991. A version of Geof Hewitt's essay appeared in his book *A Portfolio Primer* (Heinemann) © 1995 and in Barry Lane's *After THE END* (Heinemann) © 1993.

Library of Congress Cataloging-in-Publication Data
Old faithful : 18 writers present their favorite writing assignments / edited by Christopher Edgar & Ron Padgett. -- 1st ed.
      p.   cm.
    ISBN 0-915924-45-5 (alk. paper)
    1. Creative writing--Study and teaching--United States.
    2. English language--Rhetoric--Study and teaching--United States.
    3. Authorship. I. Edgar, Christopher, 1961- . II. Padgett, Ron.
PE1405.U604 1995
808'.042'07--dc20   95-12192
                                       CIP

Teachers & Writers Collaborative, 5 Union Square West, New York, N.Y. 10003-3306.

Teachers & Writers programs are made possible, in part, through support from the National Endowment for the Arts. Teachers & Writers Collaborative receives support for its programs from the New York State Council on the Arts and the New York City Department of Cultural Affairs.

T&W also thanks the following foundations and corporations: American Stock Exchange, Bertelsmann USA, The Bingham Trust, The Bydale Foundation, Chemical Bank, Consolidated Edison, Charles E. Culpepper Foundation, Aaron Diamond Foundation, The Joelson Foundation, J. M. Kaplan Fund, M&O Foundation, New York Times Company Foundation, Henry Nias Foundation, NYNEX Corporation, Helena Rubinstein Foundation, The Scherman Foundation, and the Lila Wallace-Reader's Digest Fund.

Cover and page design: Christopher Edgar
Printed by Philmark Lithographics, New York, N.Y.
Third Printing

TABLE OF CONTENTS

Sam Swope

Changing Shape and Acting Out

MY BEST WRITING ASSIGNMENTS work most successfully when students know their stories are going to be acted out in front of the class. This technique was invented by Vivian Gussin Paley, a teacher with the University of Chicago Laboratory School. Paley's many inspiring books, which include *Wally's Stories* and *The Boy Who Would Be a Helicopter*, show how children use stories to help them find their footing on life's mysterious terrain, both as individuals and as a class.

Although the production value of these performances is nil, with no costumes, no props, no rehearsal, and a "stage" no fancier than a circle defined by the students, the simple fact that the children know that the stories they are writing will be acted out works as a magical carrot that has turned even the most reluctant and sullen child into a writer. In her books, Paley eloquently analyzes how this process taps into our deep human need to perform, to see our fantasies enacted—and acknowledged—by an audience of peers. Not only do young authors experience a sense of pride and power as they watch their words come to life before their eyes, but these performances also create a euphoria in the class that imbues writing with a sense of exhilaration and fun. Paley's technique has practical and tangible didactic benefits, as well. Because the actors need to understand what's going on in the story in order to act it out, young writers learn how to shape a clear plot, write vivid action, and use specific language.

I adapted Paley's technique for my creative writing residencies. These residencies were with classes from K–6 and averaged ten workshop sessions of forty-five minutes with each class. The storywriting/storyacting residency has three elements: reading and discussing; writing; and performing and critiquing. First, I read students a story that illustrates a point I want to make, and then we discuss the story and I point out what I find interesting and instructive about the writing. Next, I give the students a related assignment—which they are free to ignore if they have some other topic they want to pursue—and then they write. (While they write, I hold individual conferences with students while the teacher goes from student to student, answering questions and cheering the writers on.) Finally, amid eager chaos, the students push their desks aside and we gather in a circle to act out a few of the day's stories.

Before a story is performed, I read it out loud to the class. (I do the reading because it saves precious time.) After asking the author to clarify the story's most egregious confusions, I ask the author to choose the cast for his or her story. This empowerment is important; it shows respect to the writer and gives him or her an important sense of ownership of the work. That done, the actors take the stage and perform the action as I read the story out loud a second time. The actors are encouraged to embellish their characters and the action, but only with the understanding that they not overwhelm or alter the story. This elaboration can be immensely helpful: when particularly gifted or even just plain exuberant actors are used, the writer often gets new ideas for revision. After the performance is finished, I ask the author what he or she might change in the story, and then the group critiques the work. We discuss how the prose might have given the actors more to do, where the story seemed too vague, or where gaps in the plot caused confusion. Then it is on to the next story.

Class dynamics, class size, the age of the students, and the length of the workshop determine how I schedule class time. Sometimes each class is divided into thirds, as described above. But other times one entire class might be devoted to reading, discussion, and writing, while the next class is given over to performing and critiquing. In a short residency with a lot of students, time is maddeningly tight. Because it takes a minimum of five minutes to act out a one-page story, and because every kid has to have at least one story acted out, I often have to work at a frantic pace. This doesn't allow for leisured discussion of each kid's work, but I have found that critiques are not nearly as useful to the children—or as powerful—as simply seeing their words performed before an audience. Everyone—writers, actors, and spectators—benefits. Everyone intuits something simply by being a part of the process. Eventually, the thrills and possibilities of performance are internalized, becoming part of a child's writing process: the children learn to "see" their stories as they write in a way they did not before.

Vivian Paley comes to her classroom with advantages not available to a writer-in-residence. She is with her students all day, every day, knows them well, and is able to draw inferences and make connections between students' stories, their lives at home, and the social and academic worlds of the classroom, impossible for a writer only briefly in residence. As a visitor, the best I can hope for is to make a happy splash in a child's consciousness, giving a pointer or two but mostly letting them know that writing can be fun and richly rewarding.

In 1994 I conducted a residency in a fourth grade class in Queens, New York. This residency was generous and unusual: thirteen hour-and-a-half sessions with the same group of twenty-nine kids, most of whom had tested below average in writing. The students and I were blessed with the enthusiastic help of a devoted and committed teacher who was nearing retirement but still very much engaged in her work. She admitted that teaching creative writing made her uncomfortable and that she didn't think she did it very well. She was of the old school, and her students' stories were throttled by restrictions: every story had an opening paragraph stating the theme, a paragraph that told the story, and a concluding paragraph. Students were not allowed to write with colorful ink. Neat penmanship was important. Spelling was stressed. Nevertheless, the children adored her, as did I, and she was not only open to my approach but threw herself into it. The school also gave the workshop an enrichment teacher, and while the students were writing and I was having individual conferences, the other two adults were available to the rest of the class.

My assignments in this workshop were often spinoffs of the theme of transformation. Most of the kids had to have the word *transformation* defined for them, but they understood the concept without much explanation. Children's literature, mythology, folklore, and popular culture are full of shape shifters and innocents magically transformed into beasts, plants, stones, statues, or constellations: Aladdin, the Frog Prince, Batman and other superheroes, King Midas, *The Ugly Duckling, Sylvester and the Magic Pebble, The Wizard of Oz, Alice in Wonderland,* and on and on. Children were also quick to note that there are myriad transformations in real life as well: from caterpillar to butterfly, from child to adult, from bad person to good, loving parent to angry, seed to tree, tree to paper, paper to art, living creature to dead, dead body to spirit. We also talked about the transformations we undergo when we play pretend—how, as one child observed, "playing pretend can feel real only it's not"—and how actors turn into characters that sometimes seem real but are not. Depending on the age and sophistication of a class, these discussions can get pretty interesting. They also provide a chance to discuss how the performance transforms the story, bringing it to life in unexpected ways and offering the writer ideas and perspectives that will be valuable for rewriting.

Early on in this residency, I read the children a story I wrote. (I use my own stories whenever possible because my personal connection to the work and the students' personal connection to me seems to make an important emotional impression on the kids.) In this story, an unhappy boy catches a fairy who, to gain her freedom, gives the boy three wishes. His first and immediate wish is to become a dinosaur. After I finished the story, I asked the kids why they thought the boy chose to become a dinosaur. We talked about how emotions influence choices, and how this boy's unhappiness led him to choose something big and strong. And that led us into a discussion of how someone's inner goodness or badness might cause him or her to be transformed into a princess, as in *Cinderella*, or into a monster, as in *Beauty and the Beast,* either of which would make a suitable alternative reading for this assignment. We also talked about how some people remind you of animals, and we played a game in which we imagined what animals famous people might have been before they became people. I then asked the children to write a story in which one character turns into something else.

One of my students in this particular residency was a bright-eyed boy named Noel. Noel was quite small for his age, and a squirmer, full of high-spirited energy. Spanish was his first language, and although he spoke English fluently, writing it was such a struggle that his teacher reported he hardly wrote at all. Here is his response to the transformation assignment:

My Father a Car

I turned my father in a car. My father can go on the highway. If my father crash it would hurt. And his color is red. He can pass a light. He can run fast. And my father car is big. And my father would have fun. And my father likes car. It would be fun if I was a car. And people were making fun of my father. On the way to the Empire State Building and he climbed in the Empire State Building.

When it came time to act this story out, Noel decided that he himself would play the part of the father in this one-man show. As I read his story out loud, little Noel roared around the circle with rotating arms, much as some kids imitate a train. When the story suggested a car crash, Noel threw his arms up in the air and his body onto the floor. "And my father car is big" led Noel to raise his arms and puff out his cheeks. And when I read, "My father would have fun," Noel indicated fun by smiling from ear to ear, a smile he managed to make even broader when I got to the sentence, "It would be fun if I was a car." He stood still during the sentence, "And people were making fun of my father." But at the story's end, as Noel chugged into the Empire State Building, the character of his father was clearly triumphant.

Noel's classmates loved his winning performance (as did I) and when we applauded him, he beamed. After offering my congratulations, I said, "As I watched you up there, Noel, I wondered: how did your father get turned into a car in the first place? Who or what did it? And why?" Still smiling, Noel just shrugged. I then asked him, "I noticed you didn't do anything when we got to the part about the people making fun of your father, but that's not surprising because you didn't paint a picture of that moment. What were the people doing who made fun of your father? Were they saying mean things? Can you imagine what they looked like? Can you tell us what they were doing so that we could act that part out? Were they sticking out their tongues and rolling their eyes—like this?" Again Noel had no ready response, but neither was he bothered by his inability to please me with answers. He just sat there beaming, full of happy pride.

The other students were eager to answer my questions, but I felt as if they didn't really understand what my problem was with this story. It seemed their explanations and suggestions were not heartfelt but only efforts to please me. I got the impression (as I often get when discussing children's stories with children) that the kids understood Noel's story in a way I could not, that they didn't require the details, the explanations, or the structure I do in order to appreciate a story. Looking back at Noel's story from a distance, I now see that it is, in its rough-hewn way, a satisfying and complete emotional statement and perhaps that was enough for the children. Noel had turned his father into a powerful symbol—a speeding red car—and in so doing he had made his father happy; so happy that Noel, too, wanted to be a car just like his father. There is perhaps a subtext here of sadness that is reinforced by the allusion to the people who make fun of his father, but then all quickly comes right in the end as Dad triumphantly ascends another powerful symbol, the Empire State Building. The story works.

Noel improved as a writer. Eight sessions later, in response to an assignment in which he was asked first to draw a map with three very different places on it, either imaginary or real, and then have his characters travel to these places in a story, Noel wrote this:

> Once there lived a king and a queen in a castle. They went on a trip. The first place they went to [was] Puerto Rico. It was very hot and they went swimming in the high waves and they bounced up and down in the waves. Then it started to thunder. A storm was on the way. They went running out of the water from there. They got on [an] airplane and flew to Las Vegas. Then they rented a car and got lost in a dark spooky tunnel. A scary looking man with a mask who limped and walked with a stick came after them. He picked up the stick and swung it at them. They fell down and pretended to be dead and the bad man ran away. They never got anywhere else on that trip when then the bad man ran away. They got up smiled a big smile and drove home. This story had a happy ending.

Noel had acquired some sense of story line, with a beginning, a middle, and an end. Using the same playfulness he exhibited earlier and a similarly triumphant finale, his writing now has concrete details, more vivid language, and a plot that is easier to act. Any actor would know what to do with this sentence: "It was very hot and they went swimming in the high waves and they bounced up and down." And Noel also knew it would be a blast to see one of his friends perform "a scary looking man with a mask who limped and walked with a stick." Performance had become part of Noel's writing process—he was now writing with acting in mind.

Noel usually wrote during the residency, but not always. Sometimes, it was a struggle to get him to settle down with pencil and paper. This was partly because of his energy level, and partly because I couldn't guarantee him that we'd have time to act out another of his stories. Inevitably, this happens: sooner or later the kids figure out they're probably only going to get one shot at having a story performed. When that moment comes, when the carrot vanishes, some kids—but only some—lose interest. I always promise them that at the end of the workshop, after everyone's had a turn and if there's time, some of the kids will get a second chance by lottery, and most of the children are satisfied with that. Of course the best course is for the teacher to make storytelling/storyacting a regular part of the classroom experience.

Michael was a sweet fat kid and always the butt of class jokes. His stories, however, were very well received by his peers, so it is not surprising that he became one of my most enthusiastic writers and showed remarkable improvement throughout the workshop. Fascinated with the theme of transformation, Michael returned to it again and again. Here is one of his later stories:

The Murderer That Turned into a Werewolf

Once upon a time there was a murderer. He broke into people's houses and killed them. Some got cut into pieces by an ax. He was very mean and fat with a bald head and a tattoo on his arm. His name was Sam. He would kill anybody that gets in his way. He once tricked an old lady. He knocked on the door and said he was poor and when he went in he stole the jewels. He even stole plates and other stuff.

One night the moon came up and Sam felt kind of strange. His pants were ripped and his shirt came off. He also had sharp teeth and big long nails and he started to grow lots of hair. He went to the woods to howl. He started to get mad. So he started to break in people's houses again but this time only meaner and madder.

When it was day time he saw himself sleeping in the woods and he said what he was doing there in the woods alone with ripped pants and shirt. When it was night time again he went to the top of the mountains to howl. When he howled very hard, people came from lots of places to kill him. One man got him in the back with a stick and he fell down from the mountains and died.

This is a vivid story, with a strong central character who is easy to act. He named the werewolf after me because he knew it would get a laugh from his classmates, but also because he liked me and I think it made him feel good or safe to have me somehow present in his story. When performance time came, Michael cast the most popular boy in class to play the part of Sam, and cast himself in the more modest role of the man who destroys Sam in the end. While it could be said that Paley's technique, at least as I have adapted it, favors action-oriented stories over the contemplative and introspective, I would argue that Michael is working through something here, and that this story does have its introspective qualities. The character of Sam is powerful and monstrous but eventually destroyed by his enemies, perhaps in a reconfiguration of Michael's own daily torments at the hands of his classmates. By casting the class' most popular boy in that role, Michael may have been identifying with the boy, with Sam the character, and with Sam the teacher, a complicated constellation of powerful figure and victim. Within the context of the performance, Michael is safe and transformed, and he has found a way, however temporary, to bring his classmates into his world—to belong.

Stories that are to be acted out tend to favor action and, children being children, a lot of violence. I can't help but sigh at that, but I tell myself it's fine. At least the violence has a joyful quality to it as a super laser-guided axe chops off hundreds of heads at a single stroke, mummies do a drop kick, and monsters eat eyeballs for breakfast. You can see the kids snickering as they write, gleeful in the knowledge that they'll get to act these things out later on. (Obviously you must make it clear to the kids that when they are acting the stories out they are not allowed to actually hit or hurt another actor.) And what their stories lack in originality they make up for in clear and concrete writing. The kids learn to think specifically. What kind of a weapon is used? Where exactly does the character get shot? What expression was on her face as she died? What were his arms doing as he fell off the cliff? Surely these skills will transfer to more sedate forms of expression.

Elizabeth was Asian, and although English was not her first language, she wrote effortlessly from the first day. The way she wrote was amazing. As soon as I asked the students to start writing, Elizabeth would tear a piece of paper out of her notebook, grab her pencil, and write. Her pencil flew across the page. And all the while she had a crazed happy expression on her face and never once looked down at her paper to see what she was writing. It seemed a kind of automatic writing, as if she was riding a wave and although she had no idea where it was going to take her, she gave herself to it completely. Elizabeth was confident enough to ignore assignments that didn't inspire her, which is what she did with the transformation assignment. Later on, however, she came back to it.

The Day My Father Turned into a Monster

Once upon a time there was a little village. There was a beautiful girl named Jenny. She was very nice to everyone in the village. She liked to help many different kinds of people. Jenny lived with her dad, Billy. Her father was very nice, too. He worked at a downtown market.

Once her dad was walking through scary woods. He heard a creepy noise. It sounded like a tree was talking. It was! Billy turned around and saw the tree. The tree stuck its arm out. Billy turned around and started to run. Then the tree caught him. The tree took a bite on his neck.

A little while later Billy turned into a scary monster. Billy looked so ugly. His face was full of vines. Then blood was leaking down his eyes. His nose turned black. His hair started to fall out. Then his eyebrows fell out. His nose fell off, too. His mouth started to disappear. When he tore his clothes off, they were full of 1,000 eyes. Then one day he just died.

Jenny was so worried about her father because her father didn't come home. Jenny started to cry. She looked at the table. She saw a piece of paper. It said, "If you want to see your father alive meet me at a place I will contact you." So she went there.

The next day the police found her dead. Nobody knows how she died. The tree got the power from an old wizard. His name was Aloka.

This story is breathless with excitement and full of sharp details. It shows an acute awareness of an audience. Elizabeth knew whom she was writing for, and she knew how to get a rise out of them. Although too shy to perform herself, she was eager to assign roles to other kids in the class. And of course when the time came for the actor playing the father to transform into a monster with blood leaking out of his eyes and his nose falling off and so on, the class was squirming with delight, and Elizabeth loved the power of that. I always admire a young writer who forgoes the happy endings so much of their literature forces on them, and the kids, too, were tickled by the death of poor little Jenny, the sweet devoted daughter who also bites the dust, arbitrarily, for no just reason, with all the gratuitousness of life.

But Elizabeth's story is also something of a mess, with motivation unclear, plot points unresolved, and details appended as they popped into her mind and not as the story required them. This is partly my fault. I was not very successful in conveying to the children the need to explain why and how their characters transform. Almost every time I asked students to tell me how their characters transformed, I was met with a blank stare or rewarded with a clunky explanation grafted awkwardly onto a story only to please me, like the ending of Elizabeth's story: "The tree got the power from an old wizard. His name was Aloka." Perhaps I am again imposing unwarranted adult rules for writing onto the children's prose. Fourth graders, after all, are magical thinkers. Life to them is often without logic; their world is always changing on them, seemingly without explanation or reason. What do they know of cause and effect?

Elizabeth's style was also influenced by her singular way of writing. She wrote and wrote and wrote, and when she was done, she was done. Try as I might, I could not get her to revise. Throughout the workshop, Elizabeth did consistent work, but she showed less marked improvement than the others. Perhaps if I had had enough time to have all the students act out both their first drafts and their revisions, Elizabeth would have wanted to rewrite her stories.

The theme of transformation is a fertile one, yielding many different assignments. Sometimes I ask my writers to concentrate on the moment of transformation, describing bit by bit a little girl's body turning into a bird, or a teacher turning into a cockroach. Another lesson asks the child to bring an object to life, giving it language and emotion, as Hans Christian Andersen does, for example, in *The Steadfast Tin Soldier* and *The Fir Tree*. Still another transformation assignment that produces some interesting writing—for students who aren't afraid of it, that is—asks the children to write about a character who comes back from the dead. Many Native American stories treat this theme, as does Dickens's *Christmas Carol*.

Transformations are something kids understand, but that is not the main reason this assignment works as well as it does. It owes its principal success to Vivian Paley. Her process takes the children's writing off the page and into the world. These stories are one way the children have of announcing themselves to the class, and their fantasies, through performance, become a shared experience that transforms story, writer, and class, creating confidence, pride, and joy.

Cynde Gregory

The Porch

What You See Is What You Get

A NEW SCHOOL, and my first day as writer-in-residence. I begin
the lesson with a combined third and fourth grade class by asking everybody to make a circle on the floor. Everybody sprawls out to
schmooze.

"What's the most important thing in a story?" I begin.

A kid with glasses perched on the end of his nose has the answer.
"Action!" he hollers. "Excitement! What happens!"

Heads nod. Yes, that's the most important thing about a story.
After all, that's pretty much what television is about.

"Okay," I tell them. "Here's a story. Once there were two kids
who ran away from home. They went where nobody would ever look
for them. They found a bag of money. They called the police. The
police came and drove the kids home. The end."

Several children roll their eyes. Others curl their lips. One pre-
tends to stick his finger down his throat.

"What?" I say innocently. "I *told* you action. I *said* what happens."

Squawks of protest.

"But you didn't tell us anything about who were the kids!"

"Yeah, and you didn't say where they went!"

"Or why they ran away."

"Yeah, and you didn't even say where they found the money!"

"You left out all the good stuff!"

"You left out all the details!"

I did leave out the details, and I did it to make a point. Stories are
basically composed of only three intertwined aspects: characters, setting, and plot. A story requires all three of these elements, or it is too
weak to stand.

Characters are the who. Characters carry the action of the story.
They also provide a reason to care. We identify or sympathize with a
character, become concerned with his or her predicament, and commit ourselves to finding out the story's outcome. Cardboard characters

who lack depth and motivation will not engage the reader, and an unengaged reader won't enter the story with an open heart.

Setting is the where and the when. The setting provides the literal background for the story to sink its roots. A richly described setting convinces readers that the story they are reading is "real," even if they know it is made-up. Richly described settings offer sensory details—a fragrance, a shadow, a texture, a sound.

And plot? Here's how I explain it:

"Story action is called plot. But if you don't tell enough about the characters or the setting, the story's action won't matter much. The plot will never come to life."

Heads nod.

We talk about setting. We decide it's more than just the room where the story takes place, or the yard or field or forest. It's the time of day, but not the hour; it's the shadows or the voices of the birds or the way the screen door bangs shut. It's the weather and the mood. Without setting, the story dries up and blows away, and nobody will remember any of it later on.

When we finish this discussion, the kids decide writing about setting would be a good place to start.

Brainstorming

I always begin a creative writing lesson with about ten minutes of brainstorming. Brainstorming is a friendly activity; it suffuses the group with a relaxed, open mood. Brainstorming is also energizing. The wheels start to turn and pretty soon everybody has something to say—and write. Brainstorming is reassuring; it offers a zillion ideas and images that spark a zillion more.

Here's how it goes.

"How many of you have a porch?" I ask.

Eleven hands shoot up.

"How many have neighbors with a porch?"

Three more hands.

"Grandma or grandpa with a porch?"

Six more hands.

"A house you lived in a long time ago with a porch?"

One wildly waving hand.

"A cabin, lake house, or vacation house you've been to with a porch, deck, or balcony?"

Six more. Bingo. That's everybody.

We brainstorm everything we can think of about porches. Jeans draped over the railing, peeling paint, a stained plaid couch with a broken leg and a spring poking through, a spiderweb, somebody's radio playing static, the smell of cut grass, nail polish, suntan lotion. Hamburgers and lemonade. Bug spray, moths, lightning bugs. Mom in her bathrobe getting the paper. A muddy footprint. We talk until our words have mingled and hugged, and then we close our eyes and daydream long and deeply about porches.

Daydreaming

As the children daydream—heads down, eyes closed, deep breaths in and out—I circle the room, asking gentle questions in a half-asleep voice.

"I don't know what your porch is like," I tell them, "but you do. You can see it. I don't know the sounds you can hear—a barking dog, a slamming door, a car horn down the street, the creaking swing—or something you can hear that I don't know about. This is your story. Look for the details. Look at the furniture carefully—perhaps something is painted or chipped or wired together or wobbling. Perhaps you have a striped umbrella or a ripped couch pillow. I don't know what you see, but you do." I ask numerous questions about scent, the weather, the wind, shadows, dishes, tools, and toys as I whisper and tiptoe among them. I'm touched as I am always touched by their trust. Their eyes are closed, their mouths are open a little. Some smile a secret smile. Some words register on the dreamers' faces—here and there, one responds to the suggestion of an insect, another to to a question about something hidden in the corners. After a while, the chant leaves me, and I fall silent.

When I think everyone is ready, I tell them, "In a moment I'm going to turn out the lights. You are full of a vision right now, and it's a powerful and important thing. But it's delicate, and you must protect it. When the light comes on, don't talk, don't look around, just grab your pencil and let the words tumble from your brain, down your arm, into your hand, and out your pencil. You are full of important things to say. Say them."

Stuck Is Just a State of Mind

Everyone is scribbling madly. Pencils fly, words appear, pages turn. Everyone is fully involved. Everyone, that is, except a few scattered souls who erase their blank pages over and over until they're covered with a smudged emptiness.

"Can't decide how to get started?" I ask a small boy with a chipped tooth.

He won't look me in the eye. "Nope," he mutters. "Just don't have anything to say. I've never been on a porch."

I know it's a lie. His hand was one of the first up.

"You've never been on a porch?" I throw up my hands in amazement. "Wow! You'll have to come to my house sometime, I've got two porches! I'll *give* you one!"

He stifles a grin. I'm blowing his cover.

"You should come in the summer, though, when the animals come around."

"What kind?"

"What kind do you think?"

"Cats?" His eyes light up.

"You like cats?"

He nods

"Got one?"

He nods.

"Got a porch in your neighborhood?"

He nods and grins, slightly embarrassed to get caught so easily.

"Hmmmm. Cats and porches. Porches and cats. I bet something happened to a cat on that porch."

"A mama cat had babies in a paper bag on the neighbor's back porch last summer!" he suddenly remembers, his eyes shining. Eureka.

"You have something important to write about," I say. "I bet the other kids will want to know all the details."

He freezes. "I don't know where to start," he whispers so quietly his lips hardly move.

I tell him my trick. It's a trick I love to share, because it works. "I can never decide the best word to start my stories with," I say. "That's why I leave half a page completely empty and start way down here." I jab my finger halfway down the page. "I start with something I know for sure should be in the story. Later on I'll figure out how to do the beginning, and I can just stick it in where I left space. Begin in the middle. It's a perfectly good place to start." The best part about this trick is that the place you end up starting, the place you think couldn't possibly be the true beginning because it doesn't involve trumpets and a procession and a red carpet, almost always turns out to be the true beginning after all.

It works. It always works. Within moments, he's scribbling, too.

Kids don't realize it, but in their hearts they always have something to say. Something big or small, important or fleeting. Children get stuck for lots of different reasons: confusion about how to begin; confusion about spelling; organization; grammar; Basic Life Insecurity.

Sometimes stuck-ness happens before the matter that is the matter even leaves the heart. If "the matter" doesn't get said out loud it gets said inside, in the most shadowy recesses of the soul. If "the matter" bears the broken-glass edge of rage or hurt, it will grow denser and heavier until somehow—through hollering or weeping or talking or artistic expression—it's transformed and purged. In the meantime, the young author will cross arms over chest, glare, and simply refuse to begin. The way to get these kids going is with an endless supply of patience, coupled with respect. Insist over and over (really) that what they have to say is important. They won't believe you at first; they will think that if you knew what it was, you wouldn't like it. They will test you with melodrama, manipulation, scatology, insults. Remember: patience. Remind these children what they *really* have to say is what you want to know. When you hear it you will know, because it will resonate the way truth always does.

Sometimes, the kids who claim their blank papers reflect a blank mind are really just paralyzed by a general, free-floating anxiety. They have something to say that is easy to speak out loud, but all the rules, rules, rules can make those things hard to translate onto the page. The words have dried into rattling husks kicked into the corners of their minds.

"What should the heading say?" a kid with a dripping nose asks.

"Do you want my first name or my first and last name?" a freckle-face chimes in.

"How many pages? How many paragraphs does my story have to be? How many *words*?" a third whines.

"I want to write a poem but can't think of good rhymes!" a fourth wails.

You Are the Boss of Your Words, Your Words Are Not the Boss of You

"How do you spell 'geranium'?" A piercing voice rises above the scritch-scratch of pencils.

Oh, no. A how-do-you-spell question. Teacher and I gaze sadly across the room at one another. How-do-you-spell questions always travel in packs. They're vicious and snarly and hard to control. The best thing to do is shoot them on sight.

"How do you spell 'hummingbird'?"

"How do you spell 'petunias'?"

"Petunias," I announce calmly. I walk to the board and write in big fat letters. "I spell petunias P-U-H-T-O-N-Y-A-H-Z. Petunias."

Hysterical laughter.

"*That's* not how you spell 'petunias'!" someone objects.

"That's exactly how *I* spell 'petunias,'" I insist. "I'm not a very good speller. Look at the way I spell my name. But I never let a word boss me around. If you let words boss you around, first thing you know they'll run riot. You are the boss of your words. Your words are not the boss of you. Just listen to the sounds and scribble the letters down. Later, when you're ready to get the story dressed up to put on the wall so others can read it, you can check the spelling. First things first. Last things last."

Before the end of the writing time, I read the following examples aloud to show the kinds of things that kids in other schools wrote about porches.

> This porch is my grandma's porch. I can hear cicadas in the trees. I can hear giggling from Mom, Daddy, Kyle, Grandma, Grandma-Ruth, and Mary. I can see beautiful leaves on the ground and on the trees. I see nice green grass on the ground.
>
> I also see a monarch butterfly. The monarch butterfly I see has huge black dots on orange wings. I also see a caterpillar crawling up one of the bars. The caterpillar is black on the sides and orange in the middle. There is a spider's web by the door, with the spider in the middle. My grandma keeps bikes and toys in a separate part of the porch. There is lots of furniture on the porch. There is a rocking chair, it is orange. There is a couch it is green with white and yellow flowers on it. There are a couple of tables. The tables [have] white pots and white, pink, and red flowers. When the door to the porch opens, it makes a squeaky noise. When the rocking chair rocks it makes a click clack noise. The

spider's web is attached to a string and a wall in the corner. I like my grandma's house, especially her porch.

Oh, and I am drinking lemonade.

—*Justin Szymon, first grade*

(*Excerpt*)

I'm on a garage porch in the summer that has three medium-sized steps. And my black shadow is dragging behind me. And a big blue recycling bin with lots of bottles and jugs. The porch is gray with chipped paint. I am ringing the black doorbell with a gold coating around it on a small yellow house. A little calico kitten is curled up in a ball, resting in a basket on a silk cushion. I am waiting at a brown door and three diagonal windows with star-like wooden rectangles around them. I can smell chicken barbecue. My legs are filled with pain from waiting at the door. I can hear the wind rustling through the trees. The kitten wakes up and rushes through my legs. . . .

—*Brenten Bradley, third grade*

Everyone is excited. They want to share, and never mind that we have exactly one minute until school dismissal.

Teacher and I catch eyes and grin. "Tomorrow," I promise, "first thing in the morning."

"I won't sleep a wink," someone says.

"I will," someone else says, "but I'll dream about porches all night long!"

And I'll dream about a roomful of children so excited by their inner visions that they never want to stop writing.

Opal Palmer Adisa

Memory Is a Cozy Old Blanket

I HAVE BEEN TEACHING WRITING, primarily poetry, to students in the second grade through college for many years, and I have found that the same lesson that I use successfully with college students works just as well with younger students. I call it "Memory Is a Cozy Old Blanket."

Although I have never done this exercise as the first session of my workshops with students, I have done so in workshops for writers and other adult participants. With junior high and high school students, I play music to set the mood, often jazz. (Quincy Jones's *Body Heat* album works very well, as does any type of relaxing music). I believe in jumping right in, and allowing students to take off as soon as I sense that they know what I expect from them. But before I do this, I like to do some lead-in discussion with the class. The amount of time I spend on this varies with the age and skills of the students. I begin by relating a personal anecdote, usually from my childhood:

"When I was about five years old I used to love to crawl under our house that was built on stilts. Often when my mother called me, I would pretend not to hear her, all the while lying quietly and laughing that I could not be seen. From where I lay I would watch the feet of adults moving about, often in search of me. One day, as I lay amused, pretending not to hear my mother calling me, I was suddenly aroused by Spotty, our cat, who was dragging a dead rat by the tail. I was terrified of rats. I tried to stand up. I bumped my head and crawled screaming from under the house. That was the last time I pretended not to hear my mother calling me."

After relating this personal anecdote, I say, "Think about all the things you remember: your name; birthdate; address; places; things; events. Can you remember all the things you did yesterday? Make a list, starting with the very first thing you did. Begin this way: Yesterday I remember waking at 6 A.M. Then string the memories together. Are you surprised at how much or how little you accomplished? Is there anything you would want to do differently? Try writing about yourself as if you're writing about someone else."

This warm-up activity is intended to get students to relax, to write quickly, and to have fun. I often do the activity along with students, on the board. When everyone is done, I usually take ten minutes to have a few students read their lists. This is often met with giggles or "dissing," but also it gives students ideas. I have a number of variations on this warm-up activity.

Sometimes I do the warm-up by going around the room and having each student state what she or he had for dinner. There are always those who don't remember, didn't have dinner, or had something that produces laughter from the group. But this is part of the fun of this exercise.

Then I go on:

"How come some days we can't even remember what we ate for dinner the night before, yet we remember other things that happened long ago, when we were very young? What is the first thing you remember about yourself? Jot it down. How old were you? Do you remember the name of your first friend? Your first birthday party? Your first day at your very first school? Don't be afraid to remember someone who has died or who has moved away. Learn to honor and trust all your memories. Think of that special person. See yourself with them. Relive some of the happy moments. Write a series of ten memories, begin each with 'I remember. . . .' Memory is selective. Because we cannot remember everything, we unconsciously select what we will remember."

Then I ask: "What do these memories teach you about yourself? What feelings do you associate with the different memories?"

After the students do this warm-up activity, I ask them to write a poem or prose piece or even a play in which they use the voices and actions of other people associated with a specific memory.

If individual students get stuck, I may say, "Sometimes our memories are a shield, protecting us from reliving bad things that happen to us, or sadness we've experienced. Sometimes our memories are a green light, leading us to a certain place where we need to go. Sometimes they are a friend that keeps us company when we're alone. Sometimes they can be an enemy, keeping us from doing what we need to do, stalking us with fear of a past failure."

The poems below are lightly edited first drafts by students from Bret Harte Junior High in Oakland, California. These students were very quiet throughout the entire writing activity, and they wrote for roughly twenty minutes.

I Remember

I remember
taking my
great grandmother to the store
walking in the store
and buying this and that

I remember
walking to the park,
smelling the air
and looking at the grass
and flowers

I remember
lottery tickets in her hand
with five dollars
she handing the money to me and
me saying, "No, thanks."

I remember
seeing her in a coffin
not moving at all
I remember she passed away
dead, gone.

    —*Brian Tu*

Three Flights of Stairs

I remember walking up three flights of stairs
    just to see if she was there.

I remember talking to her
sharing all my secrets
going to the movies
and playing jump rope

Or just sitting there enjoying each other's company
playing video games at her house
laughing and talking
eating popcorn and talking about school.

Those times I'll always remember.

    —*Danielle Shelton*

Uncle Sammy

I remember Uncle Sammy
His laugh, his smile, his way

The way he would cheer us up on a gloomy day

The way he drove his car
Taking me and others near and far

The way he danced at family parties
He danced pretty good for his age

The way he sang with his brothers
In their group, The Quartets

The way he was
I'll never forget

The way he lay so still
In the hospital, now he is gone

I'll never forget him

I remember Uncle Sammy
His laugh, his smile, his way

—*Erica Gamble*

I Can Only Imagine

I search within me to remember how it was
But I just can't remember
Is it because I was too young?

Parents told me it was dirty
Older sisters and brothers said it was fun
Everyone told me about the delicious fruits
They told me how cheap everything was
They told me it was hard to make money

I don't remember a thing
I can only imagine
I imagine trees with tons of fruits on them
Kids running around laughing, having fun

Sometimes I wish I remembered those things
Sometimes I wish I knew how Vietnam was really like.

—*Quyen Ha*

From students at California College of Arts and Crafts, Oakland, I got other results. I was teaching a creative writing class in which students—most of whom have strong visual memories—could write either poetry or prose. With these young adults I began by turning out the lights and having them rest their heads on the table as I led them through a memory journey.

"Go back, all the way back to when you were so small you could not even turn over. See yourself. Are you there yet? What do you see? What do you notice about yourself? Now what do you remember? Your first memory of yourself. Where are you? Is anyone with you? How do you feel? Find that time, that memory when you were hurt or felt afraid. Don't be afraid, it can't hurt you anymore. What is important about that memory? Who is hurting you? Why? Go to another memory when you were still a child, maybe six or so. What do you see? Are you happy? What are you doing?"

On and on I led students up to their young-adult selves. All this took about fifteen minutes, as some students had difficulty settling down at first. After I led them through the memory journey, I told them to select any memory and write, and avoid using the words "I remember." Here are some of their pieces:

I Remember

My fifth grade prize shoes. Red imitation snakeskin with gold infinity signs for buckles. I'd walk onto Bagby's playground with these on, no one would beat me. Played better tetherball on those days. Stephanie Patterson called them the "Wizard of Oz" shoes. Other people just called them "loud."

But it wasn't just the shoes. Mostly, I wore them with my polyester lime-green dress. And yellow stretch shorts underneath. Got to. Play double dodgeball, you got to be prepared. Guys look to nail all the girls, especially in dresses, just to make them fall so they can peep under their underwear or hear them gasp as they bounce on their backsides. The red shoes were a perfect target too. On the days I'd wear that green dress, with a little flared skirt, I remember thinking it was the sharpest outfit. I know the concept of clashing colors never crossed my head in the morning. This was power dressing.

Only color close to that green dress in nature is the insides of cantaloupe or those hard, bright green Granny Smith apples. Used to see them when I went with my mom to the old vegetable and fruit stand five blocks from school. It was a family operation, a covered wooden stand with lots of little areas where they arranged the fruit. If Mom was shopping for a barbeque or picnic or dinner, we'd go to Cosentino's. I didn't like grocery shopping but I'd go to look at the colors of the fruit and packing crates. And for the smell. Everything smelled warmer, sweeter as the day went on, mixed with dust stirred up from the rutted dirt area where cars parked every whichway. My treat was to strip the corn, or stroke the smooth eggplants in the next bin. Thumping the melons was allowed so I'd check the watermelons and cantaloupes. The cantaloupes looked just like tetherballs.

My tetherball partner, Grant, didn't care about playing with a girl just as long as we would win our challenges. He was my best playground buddy. We'd play all kinds of games as a team but at tetherball, there was no question: Grant was bad just by himself. Together we were monsters. Even I was scared of his hits. He was lanky, bony, had freckles and a gap between his front teeth. And he was gruff. Didn't think anyone could play better than him, especially no girl. After nailing him on a dodgeball shot, he wanted to play tetherball so he could redeem himself. We almost tore the rope off the pole, we hit so hard. After that we were friends. He stuck up for me and vice versa.

—*A. M. Hardeman*

Passed Down

Old
If you wander
Thumb   through
Ask
Truly curious
of its beginnings
Contents, meaning
Of dusty-rusty-peeling
Something   Paw Paw's
Grandma   thought
was no good.
"Throw it out"
she'd exclaim
in French.

The protest of her youngest
made her scowl just a moment
then lovingly pack it for the attic
back on Arts St. for her little boy
your great-grandfather.
Bring it down!
Move it, move it
from Paw Paw's

when he died,
to great-aunt Marie's &
Grandma's when they lived
on Marias St. in that
falling-down house
then the falling out between
Jacques & Marc.

That quiet spell
which didn't last long
(never does in the South).
So when they agreed
it would be lil Emily's
your mama got it
'cept she ain't little no more.

Which is a good thing
since mama's got
that big lap.
Hold ja in and
tell you *all*
about it.
I watch
a laughing angel
till you fall
asleep to her
voice & crickets
that tiny mighty mind
gripping tight
the family history.

—*Jennifer Cooper*

Students, particularly adult students, have thanked me for this activity. We live in a culture that is focused on the now, so any opportunity to remember, to reflect, and to learn from our memories seems a welcome opportunity. For younger students, the benefit of this exercise is that it gets them to value things that have happened to them and their classmates, and begins to give them a real sense of the past.

Rolaine Hochstein

Losses

WHAT CAN YOU LOSE?" I ask the class. They can be any age, from third grade to high school seniors. They can even be a teachers' workshop group or an adult education class.

We're already friends. The kids have been invited to call me Rollie (my nickname) or Ms. Rollie—"if you're not comfortable calling a grownup by her first name." They've written me notes about why I should pay attention to them—some notes titled *Look at Me*, others simply describing the writer's notable accomplishments, characteristics, preferences, or needs, none of them necessarily true.

I've read parts of the notes aloud and the kids already know they can trust me to address them and their work with honesty, interest, and respect. They know I'm a Big Author (I've shown them books with my picture on the jacket) and that I've come to work with them as a fellow writer. When I ask, "What can be lost?" so many hands spring up that I have to write the answers on the board:

Keys

Money

Jewelry

Homework

That's usually the opening quartet, followed by:

Earrings

Books

The classroom teacher, sitting in back, raises his hand and offers:

Eyeglasses

"Sure, and what other kinds of things can you lose?"

"A pet?" a student asks.

"Right!" I add this to the list, leaving some room around it.

"How do you lose a pet?" I ask.

Pet—runs away

     gets lost

     given away

"Dies?" The kid says it tentatively.

"Yes . . . pets die and we call that *losing* them." Everybody thinks about that and I write down *dies*.

"You could lose a friend," a kid suggests. And others tell how that happens:

Friends—move away
  fight
  betrayal

There will be a discussion about that last entry. Someone may add that a friend could even—though this is rare in schoolkids—get sick and die.

"Or get killed in an accident?"

"Right," I say and add it to the list. Now I get losses of arms, legs, and blood, as well as life. With a bit of prodding, I get:

Hair
Weight
Memory

"Yes, but there is something that every one of you in this class has lost."

"A fight?"

I write this down.

"Well, yes. But I'm thinking of something you lose when you're about six years old. You get a reward for it. . . ."

"A tooth!"

"And something else I think you've all lost, except maybe the most sweet-natured among you."

"*Temper.*"

I might get *house* and *job*, with talk about fire and firings, especially in poorer schools. Loss of *appetite* might be followed by loss of *lunch* and I'll write down both. Older and more worldly kids might bring up the loss of *face, faith,* or *trust.* And all will include *parents*, who may be lost by death or divorce. On a lighter note, a child might lose a parent in a crowd.

"Yes," I say, finishing up, "it's possible to get lost at the mall or an amusement park."

I walk to the back of the room (thereby putting all the kids into the frame) and survey the long list with satisfaction. I compliment the class on their interesting contributions. "Okay," I tell them. "Take a sheet of colored paper and a marker—contrasting colors, please—and write about a loss. You can turn the paper lengthwise, widthwise, or on the diagonal, but—my only rule—please don't write in circles. You can use any loss from the board or some other loss if you want to."

"Can I write about when my sister got lost?" one student asks.

"Sure. Was it scary for you?"

"No. It was funny."

"Okay. Then make it *very* funny. Make it *hilarious* if you can."

"Could I write about my grandfather who died?" another asks.

"Of course. Did your grandfather live near you?"

"He lived downstairs in my house."

"Did you love him a lot?"

The kid nods.

"That would be a wonderful thing to write about. Writing about people we love is a way to keep them alive. That's what fiction writers do. We bring people to life by describing them and the way we felt about them. Sometimes we put them in stories."

From another student: "I lost twenty dollars once."

"Where did you get the twenty dollars?"

"It was my birthday money."

"That's so sad. Did you get in trouble?"

"Yes, well. My mom said. . . ."

"Stop! Don't waste your emotion telling about it. Get it down on paper. Don't worry about spelling or punctuation. Just write the story. Make it as *dramatic* as you can. Use plenty of details. Let us know how it happened and how you felt."

From another: "Can I write about how I lost a hundred-dollar bet?"

"Good. Did you lose a hundred-dollar bet?"

The kid giggles. "No."

"Good," I repeat. "That gives you a chance to use your imagination. None of this has to be true. All it has to be is interesting. We'd like to know where you were and what you bet on. How you reacted. Maybe—if it's amusing, exciting, or fascinating—how you earned the money to pay up. Our only other rule, by the way, is not to write about another person in the school. And maybe not to think too hard. . . ."

But by now everybody is writing.

"Losses" is not really an assignment. It's a suggestion, an offering. In my eight years of visiting classrooms, it has never failed to elicit a huge variety of responses from students at every level of ability. Obviously, the theme encompasses a very broad range of subjects and moods. It reaches kids who have fears or sorrows to express or aggressions to air, but it also invites humor and fantasy. The choice is so individual that it obviates competition, especially as I encourage originality, honesty, and spontaneity. Furthermore, everyone is included, even non-writers, daydreamers, special education kids, and troublemakers.

Here are some examples of responses from younger students:

I lose my shoes. My dog eats them. I do not like it. He runs downstairs. We shut the door. We feel bad and then let him up. It's good to talk about your problems.

—*Lindsey Reggo, second grade*

I lost an eyeball. I liked it when the doctor put one eye behind my head and one in front. But why behind? He put a new one in front but I didn't ask for one in back. It's great because if someone tries to get me I can see the person and get away.

—*Tugdual Le Dez, second grade*

The Tooth Fairy

I lotht eighth theeff andth now I canth talkth.

Each time I lost a tooth I put it under my pillow and in the morning I found a quarter, but the fourth time I lost a tooth I didn't make a big scene. In the morning I looked under my pillow and . . . there was NOTHING! I looked some more and found a tooth! That's when I found out mom and dad's big secret. They were the tooth fairy!

—*Stephen Fitzpatrick, third grade*

David Lost His Mom

David lost his mom four days before his seventh birthday. When he came out of school that day his friend asked, "Can I come over?" His dad answered, "Wait. I want to talk to my son. Maybe later."

"David, I have bad news. Your mom is dead."

"No! You're kidding," said David.

"No, I'm not kidding," said Dad.

"But, but, but," said David.

"You'll forget," said Dad. "Go to your friend's house."

"Okay," said David.

"Have a good time," said Dad.

"Okay," said David.

"Bye," said Dad.

"Bye," said David.

—*David Epstein, third grade*

When I Was Lost in Time

It all happened one crazy day in 1955 when Peter went on his vacation to Pennsylvania in a plane. When the plane was half over Pennsylvania, it started to crash. The plane crashed in a shopping center. The plane was on fire. Before Peter could get out, the plane blew up.

The crazy thing was when the plane blew up it sent Peter back in time to the year 1892. He landed in the middle of the street. He quickly jumped out of the road. He walked into a scientist's shop. He walked over to a blanket which something was hidden under. He pulled the blanket off. It was a sports car. This sports car had rocket boosters and wires coming out of the trunk . . . [and on for three more paragraphs to a satisfying ending in Peter's garage in 1955].

—Jay D'Elia, fourth grade

I like to get lost in stores and the woods. Sometimes I get scared because it is quiet. But if you get used to it, you don't get scared. When my mom goes shopping with me I always hide and scare my mom. My brother likes to do that too. It is fun if you get lost.

—Daisuke Nishikawa, fourth grade

In the middle grades, "Losses" often elicits developed stories, memoirs or dialogues:

One day in kindergarten when I was six I lost a cat named Igor. He got run over by a car. I was mean to him because I pulled his tail, I threw him down the stairs, and I even threw him out the attic window. I feel sort of sorry because I thought he committed suicide. The day after he got hit, we took him to the vet to cremate him. After I experienced my cat dying I am going to respect animals more.

—Dave Orens, fifth grade

I once knew this girl Melissa, who bought Dino shampoo from a kid. When she went to use it her hair started falling out. She called the drug store and they said they'll give her shampoo to help it grow back. Melissa used it and within two days her hair was down to her toes. Every time she cut it, it would grow back again. She used the other shampoo again and all of her hair fell out. When Melissa went to school she wore a hat. A kid took off her hat and saw she had no hair. Everyone stared at her. They started laughing. She said she'll never buy that shampoo again.

—Danielle Triggiano, fifth grade

I Lost My Mind

One day I lost my mind. I looked all over for it. In my shoes and socks and in the closet. It was not there. I started to go crazy, when suddenly my three-year-old brother came in and hit me on the head with a book. This made my mind jiggle inside my head, and I sure felt it. Then I knew it was still there. I really never lost it.

—*Christyn Barbieri, sixth grade*

I have a short temper. Whenever I'm mad I go hyper. I take my anger out on anybody and anything. I really don't care. I go so crazy I can't control myself. It runs in the family. All my brothers have it. The craziest one is my big brother Pretty Boy.

—*Jose, seventh grade*

I used to live in Hackensack before I moved here. The one thing I lost was a best friend who I used to hang out with all the time. We used to play basketball most of the time or go fishing. I still talk to him on the phone sometimes but it's not the same as being there.

—*Laszlo Kadar, seventh grade*

The last two boys, classmates, had both raised their hands at the beginning of the workshop when I asked, "Who hates to write?" So I made sure to look at their writing and to ask for permission to read it aloud. The class was awestruck at Jose's piece: would it get him in trouble? No. I complimented the writer for his honesty, vitality, and expressiveness. I asked whether he does most of his fighting at home or at school. I suggested that he "write a fight"—in the form of a story, dialogue or perhaps a sportscast with Jose as the subject.

My questions for Laszlo focused on the friend: "What does he look like? What's special about him?" After I read his piece aloud, I asked the class what they'd like to know about this friend. I remarked that the writer should keep his reader's curiosity in mind and suggested that Laszlo try a story featuring the two friends on an adventure—fantastic or realistic, here and now or then and there.

This lesson helps students learn that writing can be a tool for expressing feelings and sometimes for finding them. It's a way to get people to listen. It's a way to have fun. "You can't do this wrong," I tell the kids. "You can't make a mistake."

Older students are ready for more sophisticated development. Dustin Izsa, a seventh grader, started off writing about his lost cat. I asked if he'd like to write a second piece from the cat's point of view. The result was "Adventures of Midnight," in which Midnight the cat describes his sybaritic life with a new family.

Jennifer Williams's first response to the assignment was a spurt of memory about a boy she'd known before she moved to New Jersey. She worked harder than any student I've ever known in her effort to bring him back to life.

Steven

When I was ten I had a special childhood friend named Steven. He was a funny, cute, short guy who came from Puerto Rico soon after he was born. He was admired by lots of people, especially girls. He was a great person who'd do anything for people.

He wasn't very good in his school work, but he tried. . . .

One day I came to school and heard two teachers talking about Steven being in the hospital because of some mysterious headaches. When I asked about him, no one could or would tell me what happened.

I never heard of or from him again . . . I don't know if he is still alive but in my heart Steven's laughter and joy is still there. . . .

The one problem I've encountered with Losses is the delicate matter of discretion. If students don't want their writing to be read aloud, I ask them to print PVT (for "private") on the top right corner of the paper. I respect this caveat, though if the piece seems harmless, I might try to persuade the writer to go public. Though I've already posted the ban against writing about other people in school, I repeat it often and try to read over the work before it's read aloud—just in case.

Even so, sensitive situations occasionally arise. When one eighth grade student wrote about losing her virginity and marked her paper PVT, I could not prevent myself from adding to my comment ("Good writing") a concerned question: "Do you have all the facts about prevention of pregnancy?" Spying on students is not my role, but if I see signs of serious trouble (for example, a student writing about having suicidal thoughts), I will bring it to the attention of school personnel—though never without the writer's permission. The fact is that the writing is there to be seen. The pieces go into writing portfolios collected by the classroom teacher. Toward the end of my workshop, students select the pieces they want to develop and edit for inclusion in an anthology.

Here are two personal pieces that were published:

Breaking Up

TRACEY: Well, I guess this is the end of our relationship.

DANNY: You know deep down inside I don't want this.

TRACEY: Then why must it be like this?

DANNY: I guess our feelings just slipped away and maybe we need to be with other people.

TRACEY: Please, Dan, I will do anything to keep you and make you happy.

DANNY: I can't. I'm sorry. I'm with someone new.

TRACEY: How could you? I love you so much, Danny. I just want you to know that I will always be here and I will never forget you.

DANNY: If you ever need anything I'll be here. And I will never forget you either.

As we both hugged and kissed each other good-bye, tears rolled down our faces in hopes that one day we would get back together.

—*Tracey D'Arrigo, eighth grade*

It's hard to be thirteen, when your body is all messed up and you are all confused about whether you are grown up or still a child. Your hormones are going crazy. Boys are your new thing. Your parents are going wacko trying to keep you young and childlike, but you are pushing to be mature and adultlike.

I would say that being thirteen is one of the hardest times in your life. You might look back at it all and say, "Was this worth it?"

You most likely would say yes!

—*Wendy Berkenbush, eighth grade*

A beneficial corollary to Losses is the way it tends to bring classes together in sympathy and mutual respect. Former nonwriters surprise themselves and teachers. Outsiders become known in a manner of their own choosing.

Taneisha Kitchings, a newcomer to one sixth grade class, did not want her writing read aloud, but I'm glad she finally consented:

Lost Family Member

I lost my cousin to a burglar. There was someone in the house when he came home. Once he found out someone was there he was fighting with him until a knife came out. My cousin got stabbed to death thirty-seven to forty-two times.

He was a good cousin to me but I had to live with it. Till this day I have not forgiven any person who has killed with a knife. On the news I see people who have got stabbed, and I pray the person who did it will get caught because I feel this case with my cousin, how I still wish a god gave him another chance.

There wasn't much to say after this, but I asked some questions about her cousin and suggested that she describe him and their relationship. When she had thought it over and written her description, she combined the two parts and confidently read it to a hushed class. Taneisha not only experienced the relief of setting the tragedy down in writing, she also earned recognition as a sensitive person rich in expressive skills, whom I could honestly call "a real writer."

> He was dark skinned, medium tall.
> He was about 25.
> He was always in style.
> He was funny.
> He was nice looking.
> We used to go to amusement parks. I wish he had stayed out for a little longer. We still would be on the roller coaster together.

Liza Ketchum

Starting with Characters

Creating Written Portraits with Children

FOR MANY WRITERS, stories and novels begin with characters as alive and complex as our friends and neighbors. Like insistent children in the grocery store checkout line, characters appear in our imaginations, then tap us insistently on the shoulder until we agree to commit their lives to the printed page.

Aristotle said: "Plot *is* character." Children understand this instinctively, and enjoy beginning their stories by creating people (or animals) whose loves, desires, passions, dreams, and struggles will bring a story to life and carry it through to the end.

I often start my school residencies by having students create portraits of people, animals, or imaginary creatures. With young children, the exercise is usually limited to one writing class. Older students use the lesson as a springboard into longer stories or personal narratives. The exercise can tie into ongoing classroom themes: a class of young children studying animals may write mask poems in which they become the animal; an older group experimenting with mystery writing may want to create detectives, criminals, or victims. The exercise is also flexible enough to allow students to describe people they know well, or to create portraits that mix invented characters with real people.

We start the class by brainstorming a list of the qualities students may consider when describing their person, creature, or animal. I often show the class the rough notes I make when creating characters for my novels, or I read an evocative character description from a familiar children's story. I tell them that in describing people or animals, it's good to focus on specific details, using all five senses, and to describe the aspects of the person (or creature) that tell us something about his, her, or its personality. I also encourage the use of comparisons. With young children who are writing about animals, I might ask:

What does the animal look like? How big is it? Is it covered with scales, fur, or feathers?

How does it move? Does it fly? Leap? Swim? Crawl?

What are its enemies? Its prey?

What does it eat? Meat, or plants, or both?

How does it protect itself? Does it use camouflage?

How does it reproduce? Does it care for its young, or are they on their own after birth? What are its babies called?

Is there a special name for the animal when it's in a group? (E.g., a pride of lions, a school of fish, a pod of whales)

Does it have unique sensory abilities?

What sounds does it make? Can it make sounds with different parts of the body? (The slap of a beaver's tail, a rattlesnake's rattle)

What does it smell like?

Is it nocturnal?

Does it migrate?

Before young children describe their animals, they may want to draw them. Sometimes the written portrait they create is in the form of a poem, other times it is a simple prose description. The following mask poems were written or dictated by kindergarten students who decided to become the animals they described:

I am a lion
I live on a soft plain
I have a static mane
I have legs as powerful as thunder
My eyes are as yellow as the sun
My teeth are as sharp as a sword
I am a lion

—*Daniel T.*

I am a furry fox
I live in a little cave
My nose is little and round as a black olive
My ears are pointy as an arrow
My whiskers are long like flower stems
My eyes are sad and droopy
My tail wags like grass blowing in the breeze
I am a brown fox

—*Sarah P.*

Primary school students (especially kindergarten and first graders) enjoy writing portraits of their favorite stuffed animals, which I have them bring to school and introduce to the circle before they write. Once again, we brainstorm a list of qualities to choose from when writing the description, focusing on color, sensory details, and especially on emotion: how do the children feel about their animals? Is the animal a comfort during hard times? Was it a gift from a special friend or relative? We also talk about the use of comparisons as a technique to help us gain a more vivid picture of the animal. This kindergarten student wanted to use as many comparisons as possible when describing her bear:

I am one little bear
My name is Carriedelle
My eyes are as brown as a stained bookshelf
My eyes are as pretty as the sky
My clothes are as pretty as a rose and as the sun
These flowers got picked from the ground, flattened out, and sewn
    on my clothes
I am as soft as a bunny
My claws aren't too sharp
So you can touch my little hand
I like to play with my friends a lot
I like to play with my little toys, too
I am one little bear
I am one little bear

   —*Celena L.*

When describing people, my students and I create a list rich with detail. A group of middle school students in Essex, Vermont, came up with the following attributes to consider before creating characters for historical fiction:

Name, age, sex of character
Body type and shape
Hair color and type (straight, curly, wild, neat, long, short)
Facial features (nose, mouth, chin)
Facial hair (beard, mustache, goatee)
Eyes (color, shape, size—and glasses?)
Smell
Distinguishing physical features (birthmarks, moles, scars)

Clothing (style and type, and jewelry)

How they carry themselves

Their backgrounds, families, where they live—are they rich, poor, average?

What inspires them? Who are their heroes/heroines?

What time period do they live in? How does this affect their lives, work, and attitudes?

How do they respond to others?

What attitudes and feelings do they inspire in other people?

Do they have special hobbies? Loves? Interests?

Quirks, habits—wicked as well as good or annoying

Do they have strange sleep patterns (talk or walk in their sleep, can't wake them, constant insomnia)?

Who are their friends, enemies, and loved ones?

What is their work?

How do they speak? Any special accent? Tone of voice?

Do they have a secret?

What about their love life?

Are they different in public than in private? Do they have inner contradictions?

Do they have pets?

As with the animal portraits, I encourage students to think about all five senses when they are writing about people. Referring to a character's smell often makes children squirm in their seats, but in fact they quickly agree that certain people are instantly recognizable by a familiar smell, whether it's perfume, sawdust, or wool and lanolin clinging to a sheep farmer's coat. We talk about texture—whether a character's hair is bristly or smooth, whether the person wears soft, silky suits or nubbly wool—as well as taste: what is the character's favorite food? And we discuss sound: the tone and range of a character's voice, his or her accent or unusual speech patterns.

I urge them to remember the individual habits, gestures, special passions, and odd quirks of personality that make a person unique. One second grader started a piece about her cousin Danny by writing, "Whenever I look at him he is smiling and what I always notice about him is his two front teeth. One of them overlaps the other." We talk about how that one small detail helps to create a vivid picture of her cousin.

When the master list of attributes is finished, we pin it up at the front of the room, where it stays throughout the residency. Some of the items on the list vary from class to class, while others are constants. Obviously, a written portrait would never include every one of these qualities, but if the characters seem superficial, students can refer to the list for ideas about ways to deepen them.

After this group focus, I give students a choice: they can write about someone they know, create a fictional character, or make a composite character by adding fictional details to a known person. I may suggest they pick someone they've seen around town who has aroused their curiosity, someone for whom they would enjoy imagining a life. One student invented a personality for a man he'd seen in his neighborhood who didn't seem to like children. This fourth grader tried to imagine why "Erving" might be in a perpetually foul mood:

Erving the Irishman

One day Erving was walking down the road minding his own business when a big black cat jumped on his head, taking the hair right out. The next day he was half bald. "HOLY MOSES!" he said. And started walking down the road to the barbershop. He asked the barber what to do. The barber said, "I would kill myself." Erving left. "I ain't going to go back there again."

Erving never liked silliness. He was a lonely man. He lived with no one and lived in Ireland. He never seemed to like kids. When a kid was around he would say, "You'd better get out of here or I'll pound you." The kid would run away so fast his head would spin and his feet would smoke.

Erving was a short stubby man with no hair. He looked like he had a crooked nose and he had very clean teeth. They were so clean, when you looked at them they would make you blink. He was sometimes nice. He had a dog he named him Mo and a cat he named Curly.

Well, that's the end of the story. I hope you liked Erving the Irishman.

Self-portraits provide another interesting option for students. This can be a revealing but difficult exercise. For those who find it particularly hard, I suggest they write in the third person, which allows for some distance, and I often use the following poem, written by an eighth grader, as an illustration. Jill has been in a wheelchair all her life because of cerebral palsy. She holds a pen with some difficulty but has an easier time on the computer. In this self-portrait, words allowed her spirit to soar, to move beyond her physical confinement:

Jill

A teenager sits on the fresh green grass,
        pondering.
Her blue eyes furtively surveying those around her.
        She is intelligent—
Her mind is filled with many ideas and aspirations.
She yearns to be independent and successful,
She is succeeding.
She scrutinizes the passers-by,
Her eyes full of contempt.
What do they know of her thoughts, emotions?
If they knew, they would not pity her.
Many only see the outside—
        the wheelchair,
    the so-called "disability."
        She has varying abilities—
        NO DISABILITY!
Why can't they look beyond?
Pity, curious stares—*why?*
The wheelchair vanishes.
She has triumphed.
She has made the world see—
    She is not a
    cripple,
    an invalid,

    SHE'S A GIRL!

Describing characters also allows children to experiment with point of view. Even very young students understand the difference between first and third person if they are told they can choose between being inside a character—becoming that person—or viewing the character from the outside. Some students like to create inside/outside portraits, writing a few paragraphs from each point of view and then picking the one that rings true for that character. A sixth grader in Charlestown, New Hampshire, writing on the last day of the Gulf War, imagined an Iraqi soldier and approached him from a distance first, then went inside his thoughts. The results shocked his classmates in their Desert Storm T-shirts, who had never considered the people on the other side of the conflict:

1. A soldier standing in a field, he is as big as a bear with his weapon at his side. His eyes are as brown as the fur of a brown bear. But he is very

discouraged because his country is going down in flames and his people are being killed. His clothes are really raggy like greasy rags. He smells like gunpowder. His friends and family have been killed from this horrible war. He tried to fight for his country and his people. He waits to die because he has nothing to live for. His country's gone and his people are dead. He is thinking of death.

2. I have failed to serve my country and let my country down. I'll wait for the bomb to drop and destroy me, at least what's left of me. Lord, please forgive me. I have failed, failed! I wasn't able to save my country. My country is in shambles. Buildings falling behind me. I wish it would end, end it all now. I haven't seen food in days. I'm surprised that I haven't starved to death. I'm a failure. No one's around. I haven't seen anybody since three weeks ago. My platoon was blown up in a blast the size of five blocks. But I was scouting ahead about five miles. I wish I was with them. They never should have been killed. I had no right to live. No right. My family is gone, gone forever. I have nothing to live for.

—*Matt C.*

A fictional portrait such as Matt's allowed him to imagine someone whose life was totally different from his own, to bridge the enormous gap between his sheltered experience growing up in a small New Hampshire town and the battlefield of a foreign country. Creating imaginary characters can also empower children, giving them a way to explore some of the pressing issues in their lives. Charles, a third grader, invented the "Friendly Monster," who helped him deal with the constant teasing he suffered on the playground:

The Friendly Monster

I have trouble at school. I usually come home bruised up. But one day something really made me jump. It was big, twice the school's size. It was friendly. It would not fit in the school because it was too big. After school when we all went out to play, I went over to him. Everyone else does not know about him. He is magic and nobody else can see him except for me. He is invisible to the other kids. We became friends. He is furry and he feels as soft as a lion's mane. He has feet like a chicken. He has a head the shape of a unicorn. He looks scary but he is nice. He's like a guardian angel. He knows about the trouble that I have at school. We had the exact same favorite sport. We both like baseball. I became good at baseball because I played with my giant friend. Then all the people who would pick on me would like me. All the trouble that I had was gone.

Not all students want to describe living, breathing people or animals. Kurt was in eighth grade, barely able to write, and balked when I suggested that he write about a person he knew or create a character for a story. He disappeared into a corner of the room and came back with the following portrait of "Honey," the abandoned car in his back yard, as full of life and personality for him as any character in a short story:

Honey

silver eyes
white   fiberglass roof
Black Body
V6 runs on 5
three gears
20 years old
Brown seats, what's left of them
No Brakes
a hole in the gas tank
2 door
three doors in the Back
But they do not shut tight
    4 wheel drive
1 serious winter tire
a hole in the left fender
a very stupid battery, it does not
    want to charge
4 Reangle shocks
a fold-down windshield if you
    take the roof off
no muffler, just a tail pipe
a BB swipe in the windshield
a radio that does not work.

Finally, students can use this exercise to work through difficult feelings about a person close to them. The following piece was written by a sixth grade girl shortly after her grandfather died. She wrestled with the description for well over an hour, calling me over once to read me the passage about his eyes, which she rewrote a number of times before she was satisfied that she had captured their intensity. When the class ended, she refused to put her name on the paper, or to revise some of the halting sentences, as her classroom teacher suggested. The process of writing the piece, allowing her to reclaim her grandfather for an hour, was most important to her:

This man has white hair. Almost six feet tall and like my best friend, my grandfather. He was so different than other people I knew, kind and gentle and a great sense of humor, with blue eyes that could look right through you, so deep and whatever mood he was in you could tell it by his eyes.

I wish he was around now but he is gone. I called him Pop, he liked that, so everyone else liked it too. His hair was real short. It looked soft and silky, with touches of bald spots. Pop had an accent from Connecticut with no *r*'s, just like when he says Go pak the ca. It is not as bad as other people's, though. He was a man that was thoughtful and caring.

When I went to visit him he was always in his garden either picking or planting vegetables. He probably did a lot of good in this world. He was like a father to me, but now he has disappeared into a world of his own.

One pitfall to beginning a fictional story with a character description is that we may come up with a good picture of the person, but no story; the description may seem like an end in itself, simply a static portrait. For this reason, I often follow the class on characters with one that moves on to conflict and plot, and encourage students to incorporate action and dialogue right away, in order to introduce the central struggle that brings a story to life.

This exercise is highly adaptable. I have used it successfully with kindergarten students and with adults, and as a way into poetry and personal pieces as well as a means of beginning stories in many genres, from adventure stories to science fiction, from romance to mysteries. And there are side benefits. When students create fictional characters, or describe people they know well, they have the chance to experiment with a writer's most important tools, including the use of sensory details, vivid language, imagery and metaphor, and the expression of feeling. Creating written portraits may also help students explore hidden aspects of their own personalities, as they take on the persona of another being, find ways to express secret desires or longings, or begin to understand people from different cultures and backgrounds.

Beginning with characters is not the only way into a story, but it can be an effective one. If students breathe life into their inventions, they may experience the thrill of watching characters take control of a story, intercepting the plot as if it were a spinning soccer ball and dribbling it down the field, dodging a host of defenders before aiming it headlong at the goal where it nicks the goalie's hands and slams into the net. In a frenzy, the authors wield their pens. Struggling valiantly to write as fast as their characters run, they chase their invented personages to the end of the field, out of breath but pleased by the way their imaginations have, quite literally, taken them over and run wild, presenting them with plots—and perhaps endings—they never expected.

Meredith Sue Willis

Mr. Death

MOST of my favorite writing assignments are actually sequences of lessons: turning memories into fiction; dialogues into dramas; dramas into fiction; life stories into parables. Each student does not always write a striking piece for each lesson, but I like the longer view and complex synergy of linked lessons. Sometimes, if I'm lucky, a few students find their way into writing projects of their own.

One-shot, never-fail lessons certainly exist, but they are most often centered on poems as models rather than fiction. I have one particular prose passage, however, that works like a poem with its powerful language and form. The paragraph in question is from Zora Neale Hurston's novel, *Their Eyes Were Watching God*:

> So Janie began to think of Death. Death, that strange being with the huge square toes who lived way in the West. The great one who lived in the straight house like a platform without sides to it, and without a roof. What need has Death for a cover, and what winds can blow against him? He stands in his high house that overlooks the world. Stands watchful and motionless all day with his sword drawn back, waiting for the messenger to bid him come. Been standing there before there was a where or a when or a then. She was liable to find a feather from his wings lying in her yard any day now. She was sad and afraid too.[1]

My lesson plan goes like this:

1. "Hey, kids, let's read this paragraph together."
2. "Okay, now write one of your own."

When a workshop is really cooking, that's all it takes. In short-term workshops, it's often tempting for visiting writing teachers to impress school administrators with lively discussions, clever activities, and writing games, but in the end, isn't engaging the children deeply in writing what we really want? Our suggestions and starters are, above all, ways to help the children get into the mode and mood of

---

1. Zora Neale Hurston, *Their Eyes Were Watching God* (Urbana, Ill.: University of Illinois, 1965), p. 129.

writing. We may be able to open some doors that might have remained shut, and we can certainly introduce literature that they would not have encountered on their own. But the best writing happens when there is least for nonparticipants to see: the kids are scribbling away; the classroom teacher is writing; the visiting writer is squatting beside a student who finished early and needs a reader.

There doesn't have to be much more to the Mr. Death lesson. To ensure that no one has the excuse of Nothing to Write About, I usually begin by having the class brainstorm a list of abstract nouns on the board. These are often emotions, but not always: hate, love, happiness, anger, depression, and jealousy work well, but so do patriotism, hope, and commitment. Also, while the students don't have to imitate the rhythms and grammatical constructions of the model piece, they should be encouraged to try. On the other hand, they may want to go off on a tangent, use this lesson as a jumping-off point for something different.

Tenth grader Nancy Finkel wrote:

Dread is a thick, black man who drifts around stealthily in the air, close to the ground like fog. He wears a long cape that flutters in the wind, which he produces. Sometimes this sound can be heard when he infests one's heart, a faint flutter that so stirs up a person that they die. His sound echoes across cities like a disease shuddered from one body to the next. He is a man to watch out for. He may affect anyone with unreasonable fears and anxieties. He lives everywhere, in the corner.

The exercise works at least as well for younger students. I remember once some years ago presenting this lesson to a class of fourth graders in the Park Slope section of Brooklyn. I knew the kids fairly well—we had been meeting once a week for a couple of months—and I did more or less what I described above. "Try this," I said, and the kids began to write. The classroom teacher looked startled—I think she had been daydreaming and had missed the admittedly short lesson. "I'm afraid they didn't get it," she whispered. "Don't you think it's too hard for them? Don't they need some prewriting activities?"

Luckily the class was already writing, so I could say, "Well, since they've started, let's wait and see whether or not they got it."

And they did. (I wouldn't be relating this incident here if they hadn't.) The pieces weren't particularly long, but the majority of them imitated the paragraph extremely well. In the three examples here, two follow the Hurston passage closely, and one goes off in its own quirky way:

Depression

Depression is a big dark being that has huge feet and giant dirty fingernails, and is weak and sick with yellow teeth and wicked uncombed hair and its head has a hairy green mustache. He looks a lot like Einstein.

—*Hampton Finer*

Love

Love is the Big Heart with red hair and red skin. He always takes target practice in his big red palace, to shoot broken hearts. His face glows and he has a black robe and fire and lightning comes out.

—*James Carroll*

Happiness

Happiness is sitting on a back of a giant dog when it runs to its master. And when he licks him, you accidentally slide off. Then you hurry to get back on by climbing on his tail as if it was a rope. Then suddenly the dog starts to run to the kitchen because it's time for his lunch. And he drags you along. Then after he finishes eating, he has to get a drink and he flicks his tail and you fall into the hole of water and start laughing.

—*Angel Estrada*

Why does this lesson take so little explanation? What we were doing, after all, was what language arts handbooks call personification. But, even with a name that sounds fancy, the process itself—giving personalities to abstract ideas—is a natural and commonplace activity to children. I know I used to personify everything from God (an elderly gentleman with a bucket painting sunsets to entertain my recently deceased dog) to the number nine (dark and dangerous, possibly a Scorpio). Emotions, of course, come with familiar images based on our bodies' experience: the flush of anger, the slump of disappointment. To see Anger as a snarling red face or to imagine Hope as a singing bird are things students have probably been doing all their lives, consciously or not. I like to bring up personification as a concept after the writing. Students are more interested in the terminology—or in reading an Emily Dickinson poem[2]—after they have actually personified.

Recently, I used this lesson with a group of eighth graders in Newark, New Jersey. The students had been writing about real people (narratives of how they changed). I had emphasized concrete details (what else?), and so does this lesson. Also, to encourage them to try out Hurston's prose rhythms, I elicited some definitions of plagiarism (Stop, thief!) and imitation (the sincerest form of flattery). I also talked a little bit about Hurston herself and the Harlem Renaissance. Since the students were mostly thirteen-year-olds, Anger, Love, and Hate headed the list of words to write about.

Some of the students followed Hurston pretty closely:

Mr. Love

So Kaleem begins to think about Love. Love, that beautiful being with huge white wings who lives in the clouds. The great one who lives in a fluffy cloud house with hearts as windows. What couple can resist falling in love without him? He stands in his high cloud which can overlook every couple. Stands watchful and patiently all day with his arrow on his back, waiting for a small couple to walk by. So he can hit them with his love arrow. He is liable to find two or three couples a day standing in that one spot. He is a happy and joyful man.

—Ali Billings

Anger

There he stood with his black hooded robe, beaded belt, and brown sandals on his feet. He stands there with his face steamy red. It looks like the inside of a volcano. He stands with his fists in balls, straight arms

---

2. I'm thinking, especially, of:

"Hope" is the thing with feathers—
That perches in the soul—
And sings the tune without the words—
And never stops—at all—

And sweetest—in the Gale—is heard—
And sore must be the storm—
That could abash the little Bird
That kept so many warm—

I've heard it in the chillest land—
And on the strangest Sea—
Yet, never, in Extremity,
It asked a crumb—of me.

that go down to his knees. Anger stands all alone. No one near him. Anger is very mad, so mad he is speechless. His temper is about to erupt, but it doesn't come out. It just stays inside because it is Anger. This is Anger, all he does is stand around and be angry. The expression on his face is unhappy. The color of his face is fiery red. He is always steamed, never happy. Anger is his own self.

—Allison Alexander

Other students, with no prompting from me, took to the poetic quality of the paragraph and wrote theirs as poems:

Hate

Look at Hate's mischievous way
it lets nobody talk and nobody play
You can see Hate on all their face
as it moves here to there and place to place.
It goes around the world and then back
making people say I hate this I hate that.
Nobody can escape the evil chill
because hate is bad, it attacks with a will.
Hate grips you and doesn't let go.
Until Hate sees that sudden glow.
The glow makes Hate lose its hold.
Now the glow is bright and very bold.
Hate can back down because it's stunned,
Now you and the glow will become one.
The glow comes close, it's white as a dove
And that glow is called Love.

—Quadir Muhammad

Hate

Hate is a fierce thing with
horns that lurks someplace
in everyone.
A demon with a black heart
that doesn't care for anyone
Not even himself.

He is watching and waiting
for someone or thing to prey on
He is eager to kill
And he won't stop hunting
Until the break of dawn

He is colorblind
and speaks nothing but
profanity
He is controllable but
Sometimes can't be stopped

Some people let him sprout
but I know through me
Mr. Hate can't shout.

—*Nichole Martinez*

This brings me back to my original point, that the compact and lyrical work best in the single lesson. I also see that I have cheated a little—this lesson actually *is* part of a series. I often use it as a break in a sequence of fiction writing lessons on building and exploring character. Such a series tends to elicit fragments and studies from student writers. They often begin with a nonfiction person or real-life situation. Switching to a single concentrated image—the face of Hate, the wings and sneakers of Love—is a fruitful change of pace. It is fanciful, yet concrete. It also offers the immense satisfaction of completion, of a whole experience—a great benefit to students of all ages and economic strata. Here it stands, the completed thing—feathered, grimacing, gesticulating. And I made it.

Rosanne M. Roppel

The Island Project

MAROON US on an island and let us write our way off," Eric Smith, a bored student of mine, suggested some years ago. I decided to do exactly what Eric suggested. I developed a six-week project in which my eighth grade students write, design, and produce books about being marooned for three to five days on an island in the South Pacific. We called it "The Island Story."

I have continued to develop this assignment and now think of it as an old and faithful project that engages even the most reluctant writers. For some students, this is the first writing they have ever completed, the first time they have felt success in any classroom. During the past eight years, this project involving 240 students a year has yielded a ninety-five percent success rate for completion. "The Island Story" also works equally well with ESL (English as a Second Language), low-level special education, and GT (Gifted and Talented) students mainstreamed in our school system. Any child can complete this project or one like it.

After a couple of years, "The Island" grew into the most exciting writing project I've experienced. Students realized that it provided an outlet for youthful and creative fantasies:

> It was fun living in grass shacks. I made a grass skirt and lei to wear when my clothes rotted off. I snuck through the jungle to hunt the wild boar. I stabbed a parrot fish for dinner, was eaten alive by giant mosquitoes, and nearly had my whole leg ripped off by a great white shark.
>
> —*Brandon Baker*

I couldn't stop students from writing. Motivating students is an exciting challenge during the doldrums of the bleak Alaskan winter at Schoenbar Middle School. Presenting a new project as an adventure helps keep the students interested and also means the teacher will be more engaged in the classroom. Some kids draw pictures of sharks biting the legs off a floundering victim in the middle of a storm; others share their new adventure stories of nearly escaping the cannibals on the island of Bora Bora; and others pine away over a loved one lost in the jungles.

Parents are major motivators for this project. On the acknowledgments page of their completed books, many students thank their parents for encouraging them, keeping them on schedule, and helping them come up with new ideas when writer's block hits. Parents work as proofreaders and as a home response group. Keeping parents involved is very helpful.

Much of the motivation for this project occurs before the students enter my class in the fall. In seventh grade, students read and critique eighth graders' finished "Island Stories." They witness older brothers, sisters, and friends working on the project. Parents are told at Open House to start saving pictures of anything tropical and to brainstorm ideas with their children for the "Island Story." Examples of last year's students' stories are left around for viewing.

One month prior to starting to write, I announce the "Island Story" deadlines in the *Parent Newsletter*, and send home notes notifying parents of needed supplies and ways to help their child throughout this lengthy project. Students read *Hatchet* and *Dog Song* by Gary Paulson; more advanced students read James Michener's *Hawaii*.

One week prior to prewriting, students watch *Swiss Family Robinson* and a slide show of the South Pacific, taking notes on colors of sunsets, food types, and vegetation. Class discussion follows and the students file their notes in special classroom folders. This project crosses many disciplinary boundaries. In science class, students study oceanography of the tropics, in social studies they study archeology, in math they draw maps of their islands to scale, and in the computer lab they type their stories and design their books. To my South Seas photos tacked all over the wall, students add their cut-outs and drawings of tropical plants and animals, i.e. palm trees and sharks. Several times students have brought in coral for a classroom display that hangs from the ceiling.

We then shut our eyes and project ourselves into our favorite tropical setting while listening to tapes of crashing waves. After taking a few minutes to focus their thoughts, the students freewrite their sensory perceptions, read them to each other in small groups, and then store them in their folders to use in their stories.

I showed students slides I took while touring and diving in and around Tahiti and pointed out:

Blazing red skies in the South Pacific, Fijian women's grass skirts sway-ing in the breezes on white sand beaches, **SHARKS**, wild boars, headhunters, historical virginal sacrificial sites, fire walkers, and under-water scuba divers tangled up with octopuses, grass houses, sailboats, coral reefs, palm trees, bananas, pet monkeys, and parrots.

What kid wouldn't want to be marooned on an island in the South Pacific for three days after seeing these slides, especially in the middle of the winter in Alaska? (If you live in the South, maroon your stu-dents on an island in Alaska in the middle of your hottest term.) Other activities keep our mental gears turning. We may brain-storm twenty-five natural hazards that could cause a conflict in the tropics or describe five different settings with colors, smells, sounds, tastes, and feelings. Everyone comes up with at least three ways to become marooned.

A shipwreck? Shot down during World War II?

A hot air balloon flew off course? A sailboat got caught in a storm?

A coconut flew into the jet's engine during a tropical hurricane?

A dog ended up marooned with his pals? An alien from outer space crashed in the tropics?

After a few days of brainstorming, even hesitant writers are hooked.

I pass out the grading rubric, a check-off sheet for the students that guides them through the project. Most students need modeling for each part of the project. The first year I wrote an "Island Story." In following years, I used prior students' stories as examples. To re-ceive a grade, students design a laminated artistic cover, title sheet, acknowledgments, dedication, table of contents, separator sheets, prologue, three chapters (for a C; four for a B; and five or more for an A), epilogue, "about the author" with picture, and artwork. The grammatical correctness of any finished product also counts.

"Is this an important project?" asked Ray Johnson, one of my eighth grade students, after realizing that all five core teachers were involved in an aspect of the "Island Story." "It seems like lots of people are going to be reading our stories." My answer is always, "Yes, many people are anxiously waiting to see your sto-ries—and it is seventy-five percent of your nine-weeks' grade."

Second, a huge calendar hanging in the room allows us to mark the stage of the project one should be at if working for a C. This gives each students a sense of where he or she is in relation to the rest of the class. Not surprisingly, everyone's birthday seems to end up on the calendar along with the dances, ballgames, tests, and class parties so students learn to plan ahead.

A third system for accountability is the class check-off sheets posted in the computer lab. As students finish each phase they color the boxes on the sheets. Students, parents, and teachers can see at a glance who is falling behind or moving ahead. To help them along, I meet with individual students to check their work and make sure they are staying on task.

Once they have an idea and start writing, they usually get "on a roll." When this happens, the teacher must be there to keep the computer lab alive:

Ms. Roppel! My printer is jammed! The printer is out of paper! I lost my story! Someone stole my disk! I can't get my story off my disk! My computer crashed!

Despite such problems, working on computers is an added bonus for the writing project. Create computer lab student "experts" for the class who can teach other students about back-up disks and printing hard copy immediately, in case something happens to their disks. The demand for the computer lab is so great that we developed an after-school computer class. Students must spell-check, print, and take their papers home to rewrite and edit each day. Pain of revision is minimized by not having to rewrite draft after draft. During this stage, we may begin individual conferences or convene to share in response groups, perhaps during the first ten minutes of every class. These conferences and response groups keep the kids on task, as does having them read their own stories aloud. To do this, they meet quietly in the corner of the room, in the library, or just outside the door.

One of the significant and enjoyable aspects of this project is when students respond to each other's work. They sit around on the floor or at tables in pairs or in groups of three and read to each other and ask questions about unclear or incomplete text. Knowing that a peer is going to look at his or her story encourages a student to do the very best job he or she can. Students are constantly asking if they can sit in the hall to read their stories to one another. Personal interactions help students to develop better communication skills for working together in the future. This is a great opportunity for them to experience group dynamics. I encourage outside editing from brothers, sisters, friends, and family, because most editing groups aren't thorough enough. Few eighth graders are capable of finding all punctuation, spelling, structural, and syntactical errors. Also, a variety of editorial responses expands the students' awareness of their own pieces.

After completing the project, students write an evaluative essay about their "Island Story." Students mention that they now realize that writing isn't just punctuation and spelling, that it is thinking and composing good story lines with plots and foreshadowing. Many have never used, much less heard of, speaker tags (the great variety of ways to say: " . . . said Bob") and characterization. Many realize that the process of editing could go on forever, but that somewhere one must stop. Some are impressed with discovery of stronger and more vivid verbs. Quotation marks and paragraphing suddenly make sense. In illustrating their books, some students discover their own suppressed artistic talents for drawing or collage. Some had never really examined a published book. Now they are noticing how many other books have prologues and epilogues, acknowledgments, and "about the author" pages. They know the difference between writing in first person and third. They learn about designing covers and binding books. Finally, they realize how important and difficult it is to be a good critic.

My experience suggests that students will not throw this paper in the garbage on the way out of the classroom.

> *"When can we take our stories home, Ms. Roppel?"*
> *"Will you let us keep our stories?"*
> *"My mom wants to send my story to Grandma in Seattle."*

Years later, students stop by to tell me they still have their "Island Story" or will relate how much fun they are having helping their little brother or sister with theirs.

> *"Have you started the 'Island Story' yet?" Steve Anderes, a high school senior in the grocery checkout stand, asked. "I still have mine."*

An "Island Story" party in our library caps off the project. We send formal invitations to parents, educators, elementary schools, and seventh grade students. Students hang banners and posters advertising the project, I write an article in the *Parent Newsletter*, and students make announcements on the intercom. Books are arranged on library tables for a three-day show. Then students and teachers stand around proudly exhibiting their books, reaping the rewards from all their hard work. After the viewing, stories go on display in the public library, the museum, doctors', lawyers', and superintendents' offices. I inform the students that I will travel and present this project to other teachers around the state and will take their stories with me. Finally, the students take their stories home.

Want to fight the winter blahs in your classroom and make your students love to write? Why not consider a visit to the South Seas to bask in the jade green waters or sip some coconut milk in the comfort of your grass shack? Let the tropical trade winds blow the frustrations out of your classroom with this old faithful.

Dale Worsley

Creating
Class Characters

Fiction across the Curriculum

CONTRARY to romantic myths about authors working in lonely solitude, writing is in many ways a social activity. Writers frequently show their work to each other for suggestions. Reading other literature also gives them ideas. The end product is, after all, an instrument of communication. While it's true that authors usually do produce their own individual works, there are very few truly original plots, settings, or themes. And as readers, we may look for artistry and perhaps originality in the treatment of the elements of writing, but we don't necessarily require originality in the elements themselves. On the contrary, we often look for familiarity there. This is not only true of genre fiction, where we expect characters to be stock types (like the "hard-boiled" detective, or the hooker with a heart of gold) and plots to proceed to predictable outcomes (did Perry Mason ever lose a trial?), but of literary fiction as well. It adds to our reading pleasure when we recognize a bit of ourselves, or of the people we know, in the characters the authors have created, and in the circumstances of those characters' lives.

In the last several years I have carried this notion of familiarity a step further by using shared elements to generate stories in the classroom. I almost always use them with beginning writers, but I have also found them effective with more experienced writers who find themselves blocked. The myth of the writer as a solitary genius has exerted a terrible pressure on many people, particularly those who began to write before the proliferation of workshops and the use of the "writing process" in the last two decades.

With my adult students, I use the idea of shared elements in two ways. In the first instance, I draw a shape on the blackboard, a circle, triangle, rectangle, sine-wave—any simple shape—and have the students do ten minutes of "directed freewriting," in which they write, without stopping, all of the thoughts that occur to them on a topic—in this case a fictional narrative suggested by the shape. The exercise often generates material that students can develop into a full-fledged story. The abstract shapes seem to have the power to elicit themes that the students hadn't realized might be of interest. In the second instance, I provide the name of a character—Cary (Cary the Character)—which is androgynous enough to apply to either a male or female character. Students who are finding it difficult to create their own characters flesh out the name with surprisingly specific details. And of course they can change the name later, though many retain it in their stories. It is interesting, in the workshops, to compare the different ways the shape and character of Cary evolve.

I have used the idea of shared elements with younger students much more extensively. Not only have I done so to generate writing, but as a learning tool across the curriculum. One particular excercise has been invariably successful, and has proven to be amazingly versatile: shared characters. I will describe the process in detail here, using examples from a sixth grade classroom, but the exercise is equally effective with younger students, and, if modified, with teenagers as well.

Begin by drawing a rather large circle on the blackboard, perhaps three feet in diameter, but leaving at least a couple of feet beneath the circle for later additions to the shape. Tell the students that the circle is to become a face, and ask for a volunteer to draw the eyes. By now the class should be pretty curious to see what's going on. When the eyes are done, ask for a second volunteer to draw the nose, a third to draw the lips, and others for the hair, ears, torso, arms/hands, legs/feet, clothes, and jewelry (if appropriate). You now have what is in effect the first draft of your class character. The students may have drawn some of the features for shock effect. I wouldn't discourage this entirely, for reasons I will explain below. However, one does want enough seriousness to get the job done and have a reasonable facsimile of a person about the students' age. It is important to begin with the circle. The openness of the shape allows the students to use their imaginations freely, but it prevents them from resorting to clichéd cartoon figures or superheroes.

When the figure is complete, take suggestions for names, and settle on one that is reasonably realistic. Then establish a few basic traits and facts about the character. Does he or she have a best friend, a girlfriend, or boyfriend? What are his or her parents' names? What are the character's abilities, favorite things to do? Are there any significant events in the character's life? In my experience, different classes produce widely divergent life histories for their characters, from sweet homebodies who like to help care for their sick grandmothers to juvenile delinquents (but usually for a good reason). Here are the first drafts of three figures from Mrs. Laura Sheikowitz's sixth grade language arts classes at the Carroll School, P.S. 58, in Brooklyn, New York:

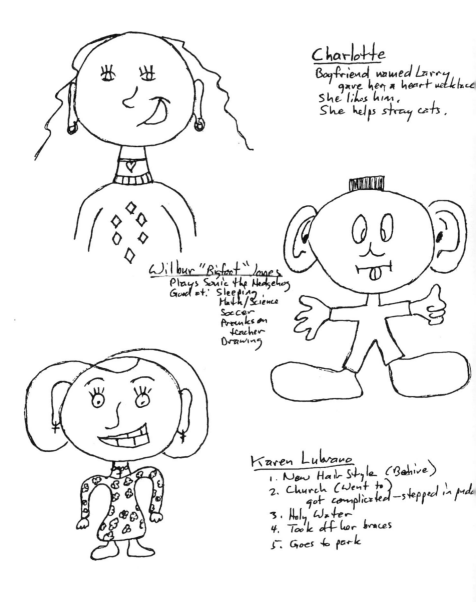

Charlotte
Boyfriend named Larry
  gave her a heart necklace
She likes him.
She helps stray cats.

Wilbur "Bigfoot" Jones
Plays Sonic the Hedgehog
Good at: Sleeping.
         Math/Science
         Soccer
         Pranks on
           teacher
         Drawing

Karen Lubrano
 1. New Hair Style (Behive)
 2. Church (Went to)
         got complicated—stepped in pud
 3. Holy Water
 4. Took off her braces
 5. Goes to park

Once the class character is created, it can be adapted for any number of uses. Students can write stories about it to develop their skills at description, character development, dialogue, plotting, and revision. They can read the stories aloud to develop their presentation skills. They can use the character as a model for their own, more individualized characters. Teachers can use the character in science, math, and social studies lessons. The character can appear in student plays. I have found that when students share a class character, they look forward to hearing other students' stories about that character, and share a sense of teamwork in their writing. When a character is used frequently, it becomes a kind of mascot, a cipher for the students that helps them understand their lives and their lessons more clearly.

The character of Charlotte was created by Mrs. Sheikowitz's group of students of various abilities and ethnic backgrounds. As a writer-in-residence from Teachers & Writers Collaborative, I worked with the class once a week. Mrs. Sheikowitz was interested in having students create and write their own characters between my visits, so we decided to use the class character as a model for their individual stories.

The class established a few facts about Charlotte. We deduced that, because she was wearing a heart-shaped necklace, she was loved by someone. We decided she had a boyfriend who had given it to her, and that his name was Larry. The only other thing we were able to decide about her that first day was that she liked stray cats.

When I returned to the classroom the next week, I prepared a directed freewriting prompt based in part on a list of topics developed by Mrs. Sheikowitz for another purpose. My prompt was designed to help establish the character's motivations: "What does the class character (Charlotte) want, and how does she hope to get it?" Before beginning the freewriting exercise, we discussed the question for a few minutes. I indicated that Charlotte could want to have something (for herself or someone she loves), to become something, or to do something. I created the following list, to provide examples to the students for the discussion:

What does Charlotte want . . .

1. . . . to have (for herself or someone she loves):
   a) an object, such as a bike? Or an artificial leg for her brother?
   b) money?
   c) protection from an evil person?

d) good grades?
e) time to spend with someone?
f) a friend?
g) a parent?
h) a pet?
i) medicine?

2. . . . to become:
   a) a grown-up?
   b) a dancer?
   c) an athlete?
   d) healthy?
   e) an astronaut?
   f) a good person?
   g) strong?
   h) safe?
   i) pretty or handsome?

3. . . . to do (for herself or someone else):
   a) save someone from disaster?
   b) score points for the school basketball team?
   c) invent something?
   d) solve a problem?
   e) feel better?
   f) find a friend?
   g) protect someone?
   h) get better grades?
   i) help an animal?

In the classroom I drew the picture of Charlotte on the board again. Immediately the students wanted to change her. Her mouth was too weird, her nose was too funny-looking, and she didn't have enough hair. I mentioned above that it is a good idea to give the students room to express their immature ideas, and here is where doing so pans out. Now that they were involved with Charlotte, they respected her and didn't want her to look foolish. Taking responsibility for changing her allowed them to change themselves, to mature a little bit. The new Charlotte looked like this:

We had our discussion about what characters typically want, and one student suggested that Charlotte might want her boyfriend Larry back after they had a fight over his having been seen with another girl in a pizza parlor. The students then did their ten-minute directed freewriting exercise. Here is a sample from the exercise, in which another of Charlotte's desires was explored:

> Charlotte wants to be a dancer, a ballet dancer. But Larry does not want her to become a ballet dancer. She has to choose. If she picks ballet dancer, she'll lose Larry, her boyfriend. But if she does not, she loses her opportunity to be a ballet dancer. She always wanted to be a dancer and she also wants to keep Larry. What should she choose? 1) Ballet dancer, or 2) Larry? She's so scared, sweat is flowing down her face. All of a sudden she picks ballet dancer!
>
> —*Luis Torres*

Mrs. Sheikowitz and I decided to focus on dialogue next. In the next class, because of time limitations, I read plot summaries rather than complete texts of each of the students' directed freewriting of the week before. Suddenly Charlotte became an extremely rich character in the students' minds. It was almost as if we had heard an entire novel summarized. We briefly discussed the idea of plot, defining it as a kind of plan or map of the events of the story; usually the events of a novel deal with the obstacles to the main character's getting what he or she wants. Then I took scenarios from their directed freewriting and we created a dialogue together, making it clear that the words between the quotation marks were only the spoken words. To reinforce the lesson, I had the students act out the dialogue. The students then did a directed freewriting exercise in dialogue.

The next week, Mrs. Sheikowitz showed me the students' individual stories, thoroughly developed pieces between beautifully drawn covers. She and the students had focused on each fictional element: the characters were complex; the plots had surprising turns; the dialogue was entertaining; the themes were deep. Our class character Charlotte was now finished with her role as a model for the individual stories. There were two weeks left before Mrs. Sheikowitz and I would be starting the poetry section of my residency, so we agreed to experiment with using Charlotte episodically, taking her into other curriculum areas, including math and science.

The project held special appeal for me because of my work integrating creative writing with the secondary science and math curriculum. (The results of that work were published in *The Art of Science Writing* by this writer and Bernadette Mayer.) In my research for that project, I became acquainted with prominent scientists and mathematicians who advocated the use of writing in the teaching of their fields. For instance, Dr. Hassler Whitney, the late Professor Emeritus of Mathematics at the Princeton Institute for Advanced Study, felt strongly that to introduce writing into the math curriculum in high school is too late: students at the elementary level need to be able to express their mathematical thinking verbally. Whitney devoted his later years to swapping pennies and candy with third graders to teach them the real significance of numbers. Theoretical astrophysicist David Layzer from the Harvard-Smithsonian Center for Astrophysics said: "While writing cannot replace the pictures you see with the eye of the mind, you can't learn to express yourself mathematically unless you can express yourself verbally." Many years ago, naturalist John Burroughs said in his essay "Science and Literature": "Until science is mixed with emotion, and appeals to the heart and imagination, it is like dead inorganic matter; and when it becomes so mixed and so transformed it is literature." I feel it is imperative that we begin the mixing process early, before the students become too compartmentalized in their thinking.

Beforehand, I discussed the concept of "episode" with the class. The students quickly caught on, because most watch episodes of their favorite TV shows. I had learned that the students were studying fractions in their math class, so we posed the following math problem for Charlotte. Charlotte is giving a party for her friends. Including herself, five people will be there. For one reason or another, there are eight cookies. She can't buy or make more cookies, and must divide the cookies evenly to make all of the partygoers happy. I asked the students to use dialogue to work out this problem. Solving the math problem in a story adds meaning by putting the too-often isolated subject in real-life social, ethical, and cultural contexts. I believe that this can not only help teach the math, but makes the act of writing more interesting.

Disturbingly, in this first episode, only four in the entire class actually dealt mathematically with the fraction problem and solved it. The rest found social solutions (a partygoer gives up her cookie, allowing the others to get two cookies each—avoiding the hard fraction problem; or the partygoers divide three cookies in half and set aside one of the halves for Charlotte's mother, making the fraction problem easier). How the writers resolved the conflict and how the resolution reflected their views of the world was interesting, but I was concerned enough about the students' avoidance of math solutions to meet with their math cluster teacher. Perhaps together we could find ways to overcome the problem of compartmentalized thinking. We agreed that there needed to be more real-life contexts for their work in math. One possibility was the revival of a school savings bank that helped the students learn the value of money, and the way interest makes deposits grow. One of the students solved the cookie problem (in her case, the pizza problem) mathematically, illustrating the solution, and provided a fine example of the potential that exists in blending math and writing:

One Large Pizza

"Ring, ring, ring," rang the phone.

"Hello," said Mary.

"Hi, Mary. It's me, Charlotte. I am having a party tonight. Do you want to come?"

"Yeah, sure!" exclaimed Mary.

"Can you call up Samantha and her boyfriend Chuck?" asked Charlotte.

"Okay," said Mary.

"Hi, I would like to order a large pizza with mushrooms and a small one with extra cheese," said Charlotte to Domino's.

"Sure, that would be $12.95. The pizza will be there at 6:00. Is that good?"

"Yes. And the address is 516 Canal Street." She hung up the phone. Charlotte could hear Larry pulling up in her driveway. "You play that radio too loud!" she yelled as she opened the door.

"So, it's not your problem," he said.

"Shut up," she said.

He walked inside and kissed her hello.

Charlotte said, "Honey, I have to go to the store for some more soda."

"All right," said Larry.

"Ding, dong," rang the doorbell.

Larry walked over to the door. "Who is it?"

"Pizza." Larry opened the door.

"Did you order a large pizza?" the pizza man asked Larry.

"I think my girlfriend did."

"Okay, that will be $12.25."

"Ding, dong," rang the doorbell.

"Hi, Mary!" exclaimed Larry as he opened the door. "Hi, Samantha and Chuck. How are you?"

"Fine," replied Samantha.

"Where is Charlotte?" asked Chuck.

"She went to the store," said Larry. Just then, Charlotte walked in the door.

"Let's eat," said Larry. He put the pizza on the table. "You only ordered eight slices!" he yelled.

"No," said Charlotte. "I ordered more."

"It doesn't seem like it," said Larry.

"Well, I spent the rest of my money on the sodas!" Charlotte exclaimed.

"I don't have any more spending money," said Larry. "We're just going to have to share." Larry got a piece of paper. On it, he wrote:

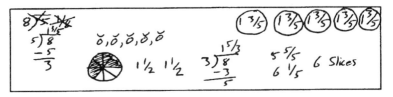

He said, "Each person will receive 1 and $3/5$ slice."

—*Laura Vivola*

Such illustrations of the thinking process are ideal ways for students to understand their learning processes visually as well as verbally. They also give teachers an opportunity to see where the students may have misconceptions, and to correct them at the source.

In our second episode, Charlotte was faced with problems from science class. To enhance the drama, I introduced the idea that Charlotte might encounter an alien scientist visiting our planet to conduct research. (The scenario was appropriate to my workshop at the Carroll School, but under other circumstances I have recommended that the students envision the class character, not the alien, as the scientist. I believe it's important that they be able to imagine themselves in such professions. The class characters, who mirror the students' genders, ethnic backgrounds, and economic circumstances, can help them to do this.)

When I suggested the alien scientist scenario to the students, the issue of whether to trust the alien came up. Some students were inclined to trust the visitor and others weren't. If the scientist asked where the nearest dynamite was, that was an untrustworthy question. If the scientist asked how nutrition on the planet was handled, that was ostensibly a friendly question. Since fiction is an excellent medium to explore issues of trust, the resolution of the trustworthiness of the alien was left to the students to work out in their stories.

We proceeded next to look at questions the scientist might be interested in: language and communications; nuclear power for a spaceship; how gravity works; breathing; digestion/nutrition (proteins, fats, vitamins, minerals); mechanics; the nervous system. . . . In one class, a student wanted to work on gravity. I asked him what it was. "The magnetic force that the moon exerts on the earth," he said. I asked if he was sure that gravity and magnetism were the same type of force, and he didn't know, but was now curious enough to research the issue. In another class, a student said the alien might be interested in how people lived. "What do you mean 'lived'?" I asked. "How they make money," she said. Taking the part of the alien, I pressed the student with more questions: "How do you make money?" "By working." "Where do you work?" "At McDonald's." "What do you do?" "Serve food to people." "What is food?" "Like beef." "What is beef?" "It comes from cows." "What's a cow?" "It's an animal." "Where does it live?" "In the country." "What does it eat?" "Grass." "Oh, it doesn't eat meat?" "No. Just grass." "Why is meat so nutritious?" "It has protein, vitamins, minerals. . . ."

Through these inquiries, the students were able to see how science is really part of the everyday life that comprises the basic content of fiction. They began their stories. When I returned the next week, they were eager to discuss problems and get back to their stories. One said he didn't know which ending to choose for his. I suggested he wait and see how the story came out—whether it asserted its own ending. I pointed to one student's math story that was especially interesting and asked him if he had thought about what his characters were going to say at the end. "No, they just spoke for themselves," he said. One girl volunteered that sometimes she would be going along and the idea of what to do next would just come to her. Another asked for help because she wanted Charlotte to explain biology to the alien, but didn't know what biology was. "What are the different parts of plants?" I asked. "Stem, roots, petals, leaves. . . . " "What are the different parts of animals?" "Brain, stomach, etc. . . ." That helped her keep going. Another girl didn't know how to explain why animals are different. I got her saying words she knew: "species," "habitat," etc. Predictably, one of the keys to good science story writing was making the connection between the usually compartmentalized science and language arts classrooms. Here are two stories about Charlotte's encounter with the alien scientist, one rather serious with a trusting response (though the trust is challenged), the second more satirical with a very untrusting response.

The Alien Scientist Episode

One day on the planet Pluto, Bobo (an alien scientist known as "Bobo the Scientist"), was having a conference with the other scientists. They said to Bobo, "Bobo, we have not studied the planet that is called Earth."

"We need to learn what creatures live there and what they do," one of the scientists explained.

"I will go to the planet Earth," said Bobo with courage. "I will need materials to take with me."

As Bobo packed his stuff to leave his planet, the others provided the spaceship with plenty of fuel and other supplies like: magnifying glasses, books about Earth, notebooks, pens, a camera, some tools in case his spaceship needed fixing, and some food for him to eat.

Bobo left for the planet Earth. He landed in Charlotte's backyard. Charlotte was in her room when he landed. She ran out of the house to the backyard. The alien stepped out of the spaceship. "Hello, is this the planet Earth?" Bobo asked.

"Y-yes, this is E-earth," Charlotte replied with fear.

"Do not be frightened. I came to study your planet," Bobo said in a strange but gentle voice. "What is your name?"

"My name is Charlotte," she replied. "What is your name?"

"My name is Bobo," he said, "but they call me Bobo the Scientist."

"What do you want to know about my planet?" Charlotte asked.

"I would like to know how people live," replied Bobo.

"People live by eating the proper food they need, having enough sleep, drinking liquids like milk, water, and juice," Charlotte explained.

"What do people do?" asked Bobo.

"Some people have jobs more important than others. Like some are presidents of the company and need to work hard, some work in a store at the cash register and they need to handle money and make sure they reserve and give the right amount of money," replied Charlotte. "Children from three and up go to school, five days a week from September to June."

"Do the rest of the people on this planet look like you?" asked Bobo.

"No, everyone looks different," answered Charlotte.

"How do you travel from place to place?" Bobo asked her.

"We use our feet to walk. But when we go far away we use cars that run on the ground, buses and trains, and airplanes that fly through the sky," Charlotte replied as Bobo took notes. "All of these need a motor and fuel to run," continued Charlotte.

Bobo asked her more questions about the planet Earth, and the next day they went to a museum. Bobo brought some equipment he needed like his notebook, a pen, a magnifying glass, and a camera. "What are these creatures?" he asked Charlotte.

"They are dinosaurs. They were here before us people," Charlotte explained.

They talked about dinosaurs and Bobo said to Charlotte, "I must be going now. Thank you for your help." Bobo went outside with Charlotte. There were hundreds of police cars surrounding the museum because there had been a report that there was a weird person in the building robbing people's money. A bunch of police officers came running to grab Bobo.

Charlotte screamed, "What's going on here?"

"I do not know, Charlotte," replied Bobo.

The police officer grabbed Bobo and said, "You are under arrest."

Charlotte asked the officer, "Why is he under arrest?"

The officer replied, "Because he stole money."

They put Bobo in the police car and drove away, not giving Charlotte enough time to say anything. When they got to the police station, they asked Bobo a lot of questions. While they asked him questions, Charlotte was at the museum asking people if they had seen a thief.

"No, I have not," ten people told her.

Then she ran into an old woman who was screaming, "Help! Help!"

Charlotte called the police and then she ran after the thief. "Stop, thief! Stop!" she yelled, but the man would not stop. After a while he got tired and rested. Charlotte got to him and she pinned him down on the ground. The police came and took him away.

Bobo got out of jail and said, "Thank you, Charlotte, for helping me and rescuing me. I wish I could stay, but I have to go." He stepped into his spaceship and flew away. When he got back home, he told his friends what happened to him over on planet Earth.

—Elizabeth Cruz

The Alien Scientist

Ding! Dong!

"Oh, hi Larry!" Charlotte exclaimed.

"Are you ready to go to Ooh La La?" Larry asked. Ooh La La was a very expensive French restaurant.

"Sure! Oh wait, I have to get my purse. Come in, I won't be long," Charlotte said as she ran up the stairs. A few minutes later, she came down. "Come on, let's go!" she said.

As Charlotte closed the door, she saw a huge saucer land on her front lawn. Larry and Charlotte gasped in astonishment. Then the door opened and a little green man, about three feet high, walked towards them and said, "Greetings Earthlings. I am Zorbit from the planet Galactica. I have come to capture you and put you in my intergalactic science lab."

"You've got to be kidding me," Charlotte said.

"Hey, kid, Halloween was last month. Take off your costume. Ha, ha, ha!" Larry joked.

"This is not a costume and I am not a child. If you do not follow my orders, I will be forced to use my intergalactic laser gun."

"Oh, look Char. The big, bad alien is gonna shoot us!" Larry teased. Zzzzz! Larry fell to the ground.

"You killed him! No!" Charlotte cried.

"He is not dead, only wounded. Now, I have used my gun on him and I'm not afraid to use it on you, Earthling. Get in!"

"Okay, just don't mess up my hair!" Charlotte walked into the saucer.

"Oh, somebody save me!" Charlotte yelled. She was trapped in a cage with creatures from all around the universe.

"Nobody's gonna save you."

"Who said that?" Charlotte asked.

"I did. Hi, I'm Mazzo. I come from Mars."

"I'm Charlotte. How do you know English?"

"Actually, I'm speaking Marsonian. It's the same as English."

Charlotte looked at the repulsive, brown, slimy monster with one eye, six arms and eight ears. She cringed.

"But this isn't such a bad place. You get three delicious meals and you get to roam freely around beautiful Galactica. Also, the Galactican men are gorgeous. See?" Mazzo showed her a picture of a Galactican man.

"Wow! They all look like that? I think I . . . "

"Okay, Earthling. It's time to deform you." Zorbit came in and dragged her cage to his lab.

"Nooo!" Charlotte yelled. Zorbit took her out of her cage and strapped her down to a table. Before Charlotte knew what was happening, she was in a deep sleep. When she woke up, she felt different. She looked at her hands. They were the hands of a gorilla! Her feet were hooves. She stood up and felt her face. She had another eye! She looked behind her and saw a rabbit's tail attached to her back. She had legs like a bird.

"Ahhh! No! What did you do to me?" Charlotte yelled.

"Ah, Earthling. You have woken up. I have learned that when you mix Earth creatures together, they become a superior creature. Now I can take over the universe!" Zorbit yelled.

"Nooo!"

"Don't fret, my pet! I will save you!" Larry yelled. He crashed through a window on the spaceship. "God, Charlotte! You need a serious make-over, babe!"

"Shut up and save!" Charlotte demanded.

"Ah! Another Earthling to deform," Zorbit said.

"I don't think so, you alien scum!" Larry yelled. "Take this!" Larry took out a grenade, pulled the pin and threw it at Zorbit. BOOM!

"Ahhh! Stupid Earthling! I'll get you! Ahhh!"

Larry ran over to Charlotte. "Now Charlotte, don't get me wrong, but you could use some plastic surgery."

"Listen, the lab is over there. You're a doctor, sew my arms and legs on and take this eye off of me!" They ran to the lab. Larry put Charlotte to sleep. When she woke up, she had all of her normal limbs back on.

"Oh, Larry, thank you!" Charlotte kissed him.

"Come on, Char. Let's go home."

They got on the spaceship and flew back to Earth.

—Rachel Maldonado

During my residency, we only just started to explore the potential of Charlotte and other class characters as learning tools and as literary subjects. With more planning, the characters could become even more effective diplomats between compartmentalized disciplines, at the Carroll School, or at any school.

Margot Fortunato Galt

The Lost Sense

ZEST, SHAPE, and surprise—a good writing exercise revs me up, even if I taught it the week before. It surprises new things out of me and my students. "The Lost Sense"—a writing assignment based on Federico García Lorca's poem "The Little Mute Boy"—works like that. Each time I teach it, I feel called to attention by Lorca's poem. I invent strategies on the spot to loosen the bounds of the normal and expected. I want students to experiment with new combinations and see the world afresh.

I also hope that they will stumble around, briefly deprived of a sense they take for granted. I'd like them to glimpse how they might cope, recognize a longing to recover their lost sense, and learn to appreciate how their other senses adapt. Although I do speak about "handicaps" when I teach this exercise, my emphasis is more on compensation than on deficiency. When someone loses a sense, I say, the other four senses become more acute. Sound develops color; you can smell the color of lead.

Step One: Synesthesia: Substituting Senses

First comes a conversation about compensation. We talk about the sensitive hearing of people who are blind, or the way sign language draws with dancing hands.

As the students identify them, I list the five senses on the board: sight, hearing, taste, smell, touch.

Next, we play with synesthesia, the mixing of senses. For example, I might ask the class to suggest a color which I write on the board: brown. Next I ask them to tell me what instrument plays that color. Hands go up, and I take suggestions: drum, saxophone, trombone, bass fiddle, viola.

Then I ask each student to write a color on a sheet of paper and couple it with a texture. Since the words for textures don't come as readily as those for color, we brainstorm a list of textures, which I write on the board: pebbly, sandy, scratchy, silky, smooth, cool, icy, prickly, rough, slippery, slimy, sticky, velvety, and so on.

Students read aloud their combinations of colors and textures when I call on them.

Step Two: Surreal Sense

Usually I present this exercise to a class that has already written poetry for at least several days. We've discussed free verse, seen how repetition gives a song-like quality to a poem, and considered the virtues of compression and surprise. They know that poetry comes from real life but transforms experience by, among other things, comparisons.

Now I explain that the poem I'm about to read by the Spanish poet Federico García Lorca departs from real life in radical ways. It enters a surreal realm: *surreal* means above the real, beyond the real.

I mention Salvador Dali. "He painted pictures of clocks dripping over walls to suggest how slow time feels when you're bored. Lorca's poem has some very odd ideas, but on inspection, you'll see that they work just like Dali's limp clocks."

Before I read the poem, I also discuss what a translation means and tell them that W. S. Merwin translated this Lorca poem from the Spanish.

The poem has parentheses, too, I tell the students, and ask them when you're supposed to use parentheses. "To set something off that's private," they'll say. "Or to add a thought that isn't in the main line of thinking." Acknowledging the correctness of these answers, I suggest that Lorca uses parentheses in radical ways, to capture another version of reality and enter it into the story of the poem. I promise to cup my hands to show when the parentheses come.

Here is the poem:

The Little Mute Boy

The little mute boy was looking for his voice.
(The king of the crickets had it.)
In a drop of water
the little boy was looking for his voice.

I do not want it for speaking with:
I will make a ring of it
so that he may wear my silence
on his little finger.

In a drop of water
the little boy was looking for his voice.

(The captive voice, far away,
put on a cricket's clothes.)

There's a lot going on in this little poem. The surreal elements occur in the imaginative leaps and the metaphor for loss that Lorca creates. For example, on first glance it's odd to think of looking for a voice in a drop of water. Why would a lost voice gravitate toward water? Before answering this, we discuss what *mute* means and what things in the poem have voices, though not in the usual sense.

Water has a voice, a drop of water has a voice. We brainstorm different voices of water: raindrops, a dripping tap, waves lapping or crashing, a brook gurgling, water splashing around a car, the clunk or tinkle of an ice cube in a glass, the hiss of steam. So it's not so odd, after consideration, that the little boy looks for his voice in a drop of water. Water has so many voices, his might have gotten mixed in by mistake.

Crickets also have voices. Most city children don't know that you rarely see crickets, but you hear them. A cricket trapped in a room can sound like a conductor tuning up an invisible orchestra. So, it's not so surprising that the king of the crickets might steal the little boy's voice. (Speaking of the cricket king, Lorca created a fairy-tale aura, similar to that of some of the biomorphic creatures that artists such as Joan Miró and Paul Klee created. Students might enjoy giving names to some of the creatures in works by these artists.)

I ask the children to imagine reasons why the cricket king would steal a human voice. (This empathy gets them ready to imagine what it would be like themselves to live without one of their senses.) Maybe he's tired of his own chirp; maybe his own child was born mute and he couldn't find a cricket to give up a voice; maybe the king is making a collection of beautiful voices from all over the world, and the boy's caught his ear. When at the end of the poem, the captive voice puts on the cricket's clothes, what motive for the theft becomes more likely?

The second stanza in the poem is even more odd than the others. Here somebody speaks of making a ring out of the voice so that "he may wear my silence on his little finger." This shift in voice and point of view may slip right by some students, and it's up to the teacher to decide whether to stop and discuss it or not. It is probably the boy who is speaking to the thief, but it is also possible that it is the thief who is speaking. I like the ambiguity here because it draws us into a deeper understanding of how we label a handicap a deficiency rather than recognizing its status as a beautiful, rare exception.

Step Three: Life without a Sense

Since most of us take our senses for granted, I want students to brainstorm some personal reactions to losing one of their senses. To begin, I ask each student to decide which sense they are willing to relinquish for the duration of the poem, and to write this sense at the top of their paper. It is interesting how many of them choose taste or smell, almost as though they're unwilling even to play with the possibility of losing sight, hearing, or touch. It is worthwhile to discuss these choices with the class, and to investigate why we rely so much on sight, hearing, and touch. It helps make them more appreciative of the gifts these senses bring, and sympathetic to those who live without them.

After everyone has chosen a sense to lose, I ask them to write down what they would miss most from this sense. Many will write "the taste of pizza." Red, spicy, gooey foods appeal mightily to fourth graders.

Next, I ask them to consider how losing this sense might endanger them: unable to feel a hot stove, or to hear an oncoming train.

What would confuse you or what would you be unable to do, if you lost your sense? I ask next. Couldn't tell hot peppers from cold milk. Couldn't tell if my socks matched or if I pulled the cereal box I want from the shelf.

If you lost your sense, what would be the benefits? Wouldn't have to smell rotted garbage in summer. Or feel sweaty hands when you shake hands with one of your parents' friends. Wouldn't have to listen to your sister play the trombone.

Step Four: Creating a Net of Surprises

Robert Frost's description of free verse as playing tennis without a net set me thinking about ways to create forms that will surprise young writers to do things they wouldn't normally attempt. Or, to think of it another way, I want to rub rules against their imaginations to light a fire in the shape of a song.

For this exercise, the net I create with the class is based on guided associations. It works like this:

—Each student writes a list of words.

—The list is individual in substance yet general in categories.

—I create the categories on the spur of the moment, but I am guided by the notion of travel or a journey, and so I usually include some items of travel paraphernalia (something like a map, maybe) and some element of geography (like a continent, ocean, etc.). I also want to encourage synesthesia, and so will pair categories, saying, for example, "A Color," and next, "The Texture of That Color."

Next, I explain that I will say a category and they will write a specific item in that category.

Here are the categories I used recently with a fourth grade class:

—an item of clothing
—a unusual color from the sixty-four color Crayola box
—a sound in nature that fits this color
—a continent or country or place
—a texture

And here are several lists:

—a cape
—burnt sienna
—pigeon's cooing
—Mexico
—splintery

    —M. F. G.

—quilt
—red
—fire
—China
—soft

    —A student

—boots
—magenta
—surf crashing
—bayou
—fluffy

    —A teacher

Step Five: Writing a Poem of Searching for a Lost Sense

Getting the class ready to write their own poems, I reread Lorca's poem aloud and mention some of the strategies he uses. I write these on the board:

—The parentheses that give away clues or the actual location of the lost sense.

—Repetition of lines that talk about searching.

—Looking in unusual places that turn out to have some connection to the sense.

—A wish to do something with the sense that might emphasize its loss or how much you miss it.

—What the lost sense does without you.

I also emphasize writing about how you would compensate without the sense:

"Tongue, now that you're swallowed
I must sniff myself through
a pizza . . .

The sky has the color of cymbals
now that blue has drowned

A rose petal against my face
smells like a tickling kiss . . . "

"Remember," I remind the students, "you're on a journey to find your lost sense. Think of various ways to travel, think of oceans, glaciers, deserts, rivers, bridges, crossroads, or small spaces like stairs, drawers, closets, pockets, toothpaste tubes, clockfaces."

Finally come the instructions about the net of words: "*You must use every word on your list in the order they're written.*" Then I take the last part back: "*But if you must move them around, you can.*" Don't be afraid to make all kinds of leaps in sense, and at the same time think about the way your lost sense would operate if it were really lost. Where would it go? How would it react to your calling it? How would it like to be cornered and captured? Does it miss you too? Has it changed into something else?

Step Six: Writing and Reading
I write along with the students for about five minutes, usually explaining that I'll do that and then help them afterward. My last words of encouragement before I pick up the chalk for my own poem are: "You don't have to know where this poem will take you when you start. Use

your first word and think of some connection between it and your
search or your lost sense, then move on to other strategies we've
listed."

Here's a fragment of a poem I wrote about my lost taste:

Taste has left its cape
in my closet, then
disappeared in its folds.
Pizza flops on my tongue
like a left over tail.
Burnt sienna flavors
every meal with its
pigeon's coo.
How I miss
splintery celery
pebbly cookie.
Meanwhile, my taste,
swashbuckler of meals,
forks its way across
the border. Sends me
a postcard on a chili:
"Amigo, look for me
under the sombrero
of a nose, in a
mountain of tacos."
Rascal, I know him
watering his bushes,
a figment of teeth,
a jouster of corn.

Here are some poems by fourth grade students and one by their
teacher Judith Pfeifer, from Pine Hill Elementary, Cottage Grove,
Minnesota:

Sense of Sight

I can't see what I'm trying
to find. I am trying
to find my quilt.
If I find it I will
use it to keep me warm
in the winter. It's soft
as a baby's skin. If I
don't find it I will
find fire red as the sun.

I will go to China to find
a dragon that can blow
fire or it might
have my quilt. I
will listen to the
hot fire.

    —Larry Hui

I have no sense of taste.
I have been looking for
it. Little Swedish spike-headed
ants have taken
my taste. It is calling
out to me, it sounds like
a dripping faucet when
it yells. It is held
captive in a brick red
blob which has a big
fat coat in it.

    — Jeff Hillyer

A parka was sitting on the table
when I went to put it on
I lost my taste.
That day everything I ate
didn't taste.
I wondered about pop, so I
bought root beer. Still
no taste, but they
gave me a green harmonica.
Did my taste go to Greenland or Texas?
Just tell me where he went!
Then five years later I ate some pizza
and finally found him.

    — Kyle Magyar

I'm looking for my sense of hearing.
How can I find it without
being able to hear?
I already looked in Florida,
in someone else's shoes.
I followed a yellow bee flying
in the air.

I felt something as
sandy
as sandpaper.
Oh where Oh where is my
sense of hearing?
How I miss being able
to hear the bees buzzing
and the color blue
sounding like a trumpet.
I also miss talking
on the phone.

    —*Conrad La Doux*

Hearing flows out of me through
the warm soles of my cowboy boots.
My own footfalls on the stairs
are strangely silent.

The magenta sunrise reflects
on the surf slamming
soundlessly against the rocks.

My parrot's fluffy feathers rise
in frustration as his whole body
strains, shrieking unheard on top
of his cage.

My coffee maker drips but only
the light tells when it is ready.
Its final "thunks" are gone.

As I leave to search for sound
at school, the door slams shut
behind me but the bang is missing.

The key turns in the ignition.
I wait trying to feel the car's vibration.
It shudders, I hope it will
move as I shift and step
on the accelerator.

Children come at me, eyes wide
and lips moving. Their crucial
messages are empty holes
in the air.

Desks scrape across the floor
unheard. Children move their
mouths at each other appearing
fascinated by facial movements.

Suddenly I hear a whisper.
The heating unit fan kicks in.
Reality returns with a rush
of classroom cacophony.
I consider the pros and cons.

  —Judith Pfeifer

David Mills

My Magic Hands

M Y MAGIC HANDS" is one of my favorite writing assignments for
secondary school kids. Because I am a young black male, and there
are not enough of us teaching in the public schools, I try to use poems
that reflect the sounds of the city, something that comes out of the
kids' cultural grab bag. Sometimes I get the feeling, certainly with
poetry, that kids of color in inner-city public schools do not think that
people of color write poetry. One of my missions is to show these kids
that not only do we write, we write in many different voices, from
formalist to hip-hop.

To this end I almost always use poets of color as my examples,
first giving the students some background on the writer. One writer I
am a big fan of is a newcomer to the poetry scene, Paul Beatty. I use
one of his poems, "Gription," as a jumping-off point for "My Magic
Hands."

Because I am both a writer and an actor, I like to bring poetry
into the bodies and mouths of the students. Beatty's poem helps do
this by the way it uses personification, slang, internal rhyme, and off-
rhyme. (By the time I bring in this assignment, I have already talked
with the students about the uses and misuses of exact rhyme.)

I start off by asking students to off-rhyme. I ask one student to
make up a line such as "the sky's eyes are red," and then I ask another
student to off-rhyme with that line. Another student might come up
with something like: "Because it always holds its breath." I have students do these off-rhyme couplets all the way around the room. I do
this because it brings poetic language to the body, to the mouth.

I then discuss personification. I give the students an example of
personification such as "the sea kissed the shore," and ask the students
what is the human thing in that phrase. "The kissing." Then I ask for
other examples of personification.

By asking the kids about their hands, I shift the discussion in the
direction of Beatty's poem: "Touch your hands, what do they feel like?
What do they look like? What do you do with them?" Answers run
the gamut from the mundane to the lewd. I'm sure you can imagine

what some pubescent boys might say. If a student says his or her hands can make beats, I ask that student to bang on a table, create a rhythm. I then ask that student how his or her hands feel when they do this. I ask all the students to clap their hands. "How do your palms feel?" Some of their eyes light up when they realize that their hands feel hot or tingly.

Then I pass out Beatty's poem. I ask a student to read it aloud.

Gription

wuddup
whaz hat-nen
you man

       two nigguh
       hands swing

in mid arc
fingers hesitate
wait   is he bringin
that ol school soulshake
or he gonna skip step 2
do a quick slide n glide
          hope he dont trip
          and go into
          all that post grip
          flip wilson
          royal order of the
          water buffalo shit
       finger snappin
     hand clappin
   elbow taps
twists

then i'll improvise
my handshake guise
and just bang fists

Beatty's language is very energetic, combining academic jargon and inner-city argot. Oftentimes students look at the first couple of words—"wuddup" and "whaz hat-nen"—and they recoil, or the syllables come out of their mouths as if their minds are stuck in first gear. A student will often say, "Those aren't words."

"What do you say to your boys when you first see them?"

"What's up?"

"So what do you think is on that piece of paper?"

"'Wuddup,' but that's not how you spell it."

"But that is the way a lot of you pronounce it."

A little smile crawls across their faces as they realize that Beatty might be one of them.

Once the student finishes reading the poem aloud, I ask what it's about. Many of the students assume it's some sort of fight because of the allusion to the hands. Then I ask them to look again.

Because of my belief that poetry comes from the body, I get two volunteers to act out the poem. I say to one student, "Walk in and say 'Wuddup.'" She does. I ask the other student to say, "Whaz hat-nen." He does. Then I ask the first student to say, "You man," she does. Then I say, "I want the two of you to dramatize the rest of what I read. 'Two nigguh hands swing in mid arc.' What's an arc?" Invariably, some student will say, "Noah's boat!"

"Think math."

"Oh, it's part of a circle." So I ask my volunteers to make a circular movement with their arms—bringing their arms back like a bowler at the high point of the backswing. The next line is, "fingers hesitate." "What does *hesitate* mean?"

"To stop." So I stop my two volunteers before they slap five. Then we continue with the poem: "wait is he bringin / that ol school soulshake / or he gonna skip step 2 / do a quick slide n glide." I ask one of the volunteers to moonwalk like Michael Jackson—talk about a funny and embarrassing moment—watching some ungainly student moonwalk. "Hope he dont trip / and go into / all that post grip / flip wilson / royal order of the / water buffalo shit"—I usually erase the word "shit" before I xerox and hand out the poem—"finger snappin" (I ask that same volunteer to snap his fingers); "hand clappin" (I ask the student to clap his or her hands); "elbow taps" (I ask them to tap their elbows—this last request usually gets me an urban adaptation of Daniel Day Lewis's performance in *My Left Foot*). At "twists" I ask that same student to do the twist (most of them aren't hip to Chubby Checker; he's about Noah's age in their minds). "Then I'll improvise / my handshake guise / and just bang fists." I ask the two students to bang fists.

"What is the poem about?" Big lightbulb goes on, "Oh, it's about giving someone grip. Oh that's fly!"

"What about the title, 'Gription'?" What do you think that means?"

"It's about giving grip."

"Yeah, and if something is not fact, it is what?"

"It's a lie."

"Or?"

"It's *fiction!*"

"*Grip* plus *fiction* equals *gription.*"

"So it's like a made-up story about giving grip." The kids really gravitate towards the poem because Beatty has taken something from their everyday lives—a handshake—and made poetry out of it.

I thank my two volunteers and they pop a squat. I ask the students what they think an "ol school soulshake" is: "What did they do back when your grandmother was a kid?"

"Slap five!"

"There you go. Who is Flip Wilson?" I have taught this poem at more than thirty schools and I have gotten only one correct answer to this question. When students don't have the answer I help them. "How many of you watch Martin?"

"Yeah!"

"Who says, 'You so crazy'?"

"Sha ne ne!"

"Well, Flip Wilson is a comedian who had a TV show in the sixties and seventies. He, like Martin, had a female alter ego named Geraldine. And Wilson used to dress up like a woman and carry on like Martin does. Matter of fact, Martin might have gotten Sha ne ne from Flip." I know some of us who were born before the Flood—as far as the students are concerned—might also remember Milton Berle's cross-dressing. But one example is enough. Then I ask about the lines, "royal order of the / water buffalo." Hollywood is a blessing in disguise. A lot of kids are able to pick up that Flintstones allusion because of the film. "Why do you think Beatty would allude to the Flintstones in his poem?"

"I don't know."

"What did they do at the Water Buffalo Lodge?" Light bulb three: "A secret handshake!"

"And what is this poem about?"

"Grip!"

"What does 'improvise' mean?"

Occasionally I'll get a correct answer. But if not I can make a connection with pop culture. "What does a freestyle rapper do?"

"He makes up rhymes off the top of his head."

"Well that's what improvisation is, to make it up on the spot. What does guise mean?"

"Boys, dummy."

"Look at the way it's spelled."

"I don't know."

"How do some boys wear their jeans nowadays?"

"They wear them baggy."

"What do you call that?"

"It's a style."

"Well, that's what a guise is."

I ask where the personification in the poem is. It takes them a few minutes. But inevitably a student says, "It's as if the fingers are talking when the poem says "fingers hesitate / wait   is he bringin / that ol school. . . .""

"That's it."

Then I ask them to do the unthinkable: take out a sheet of paper and spread one hand on the sheet of paper and outline it. This request inevitably meets with the derisive comment: "I did this in second grade!" Then I ask them to write a poem in the outlines of their hands about something they do with their hands.

My only restriction is that they not start out with "I use my hands to do. . . ." I say, "Look at Beatty's poem. He is in the moment. The poem is about a type of handshake and he has us right in the moment of a handshake rather than setting us up for it. He doesn't say, 'I use my hands to give grip.'"

"Do you think the two people in this poem know each other?"

"Yes."

"Do you think they have been hanging around each other all day? Look at the first two words."

"No, because they are saying 'wuddup,' like hello."

My other suggestion is not to worry about whether or not they can pull off internal or off-rhyme like Beatty. I also tell them that if they can get some personification in, that would be nice. And use detail. That's what makes you you.

Master Scratch

I scratch records
They feel smooth. I move
My hands back
And forth making music

   —Bolfie

My Middle Finger

I use it to express
Myself when I get
Upset

   —William Colon

Source

Paul Beatty, "Gription," from *Big Bank Take Little Bank* (New York: The Nuyorican Poets Cafe, 1991).

Elizabeth Raby

Sweeping Hearts
Writing Poems Inspired by Native American Music & Poetry

HAVING STUDENTS write poems while listening to a cassette tape of "Earth Spirit" by R. Carlos Nakai, a Navajo-Ute who plays the Native American flute, has been a remarkably successful exercise with young people from grades two through twelve. Inspired in part by the Native American poets at the 1988 and 1992 Geraldine R. Dodge Poetry Festivals at Hopewell, N. J., and in part by Margot Fortunato Galt's article, "The Story in History," in the September–October 1992 issue of *Teachers & Writers*, I use the tape as a way to bring a Native American presence to the classrooms I visit as a poet-in-the-schools in New Jersey and Pennsylvania.

Following Galt's example, I draw both a pyramid and a circle on the chalkboard. Galt says that the European conception of the universe is structured like a pyramid, by which things are ranked "according to their smartness or complexity or similarity to us." On this pyramid, humans are outranked only by the angels and then by God. Students have little difficulty assigning things to a place in this hierarchy. I suggest that dirt may rank near the bottom, hence our tendency to feel justified in treating dirt "like dirt." Students find it easy to think of examples of what we have done to dirt.

We next consider the Native American paradigm of being: a circle that includes, in no hierarchical order, humans and dirt, thunder and bears. I read aloud Joy Harjo's "Eagle Poem," a fine example of the circularity and the respect for the things of this world that such a vision engenders:

> To pray you open your whole self
> To sky, to earth, to sun, to moon,
> To one whole voice that is you.
> And know that there is more
> That you can't see, can't hear,
> Can't know except in moments

Steadily growing, and in languages
That aren't always sound but other
Circles of motion.
Like eagle that Saturday morning
Over Salt River. Circled in blue sky
In wind, swept our hearts clean
With sacred wings.
We see you, see ourselves and know
That we must take the utmost care
And kindness in all things.
Breathe in, knowing we are made of
All this, and breathe, knowing
We are truly blessed because we
Were born, and die soon within a
True circle of motion,
Like eagle rounding out the morning
Inside us.
We pray that it will be done
In beauty.
In beauty.

With this poem still echoing in our minds, I tell the class that we will write while listening to a tape of Native American flute music. After making sure that everyone has paper and a sharpened pencil, I explain that while the tape plays I will read three poems aloud, and that afterward there should be no talking for a few minutes. The only sound will be the sound of the flute. I invite the students to go wherever the flute takes them, to hear whatever message it brings them, to follow whatever story it tells—to write down whatever comes to them.

The first poem I read is "Spring Night in Lo-Yang—Hearing a Flute" by Li Po, which I tell the students was written more than a thousand years ago:

In what house, the jade flute that sends these dark notes drifting,
scattering on the spring wind that fills Lo-Yang?
Tonight if we should hear the willow-breaking song,
who could help but long for the gardens of home?

    —Translated by Burton Watson

Then I read Joy Harjo's "Song for the Deer and Myself to Return On":

This morning when I looked out the roof window
before dawn and a few stars were still caught

in the fragile weft of ebony night
I was overwhelmed. I sang the song Louis taught me:
a song to call the deer in Creek, when hunting,
and I am certainly hunting something as magic as deer
in this city far from the hammock of my mother's belly.
It works, of course, and deer came into this room
and wondered at finding themselves
in a house near downtown Denver.
Now the deer and I are trying to figure out a song
to get them back, to get us all back,
because it's too early to call Louis
and nearly too late to go home.

Finally, I read "An Evening at Windy Point for Christopher Jay"
by the Hopi poet, Ramson Lomatewama. It begins with the sound of
a Japanese bamboo flute (*suizen*):

The sound of suizen
lingers over a valley of sand.
Desert shadows grow in silence.
The man, sitting at the edge,
brings music to Windy Point.
Below,
juniper and piñon trees listen.
Smooth bamboo songs
touch the face of summer.
There are no monastery walls here,
Only the music,
the man,
the spirit.

The haunting sound of the flute and the softly spoken poems have
never failed to achieve a strange combination of attention and peace-
fulness in the classroom. Very young children may miss an occasional
word or reference, they never miss the beauty of the language or the
spirit of the poems. Usually there is so much noise in our lives—perhaps without realizing it we all hunger for the calm this music inspires.
Students often ask that it be played as the background to other writing exercises. The music establishes a mood they like to extend, which
makes it especially good for the first day of a writing workshop.

The music evokes strong emotions in the students, makes them
wish for a more perfect world, and gives many of them a chance to
express their anguish and anger about the state of the environment.
They take bits and pieces from the poems I read aloud and combine

them with their own personal histories and the mood the music creates. Here are some examples:

Watching Wondering

I wake and hear the sweet music of the flute
I follow it
    Watching
        Wondering
Beauty fills the air
Each step I take
    Watching
        Wondering
Suddenly the music gets louder
I spot a giant fall of water
    Watching
        Wondering
The lion was next to the lamb
There meadows and lakes are plenty
    Watching
        Wondering
I sit under a tree thinking
Has God called me home?
    Watching
        Wondering.
I close my eyes and fall asleep
    Watching and
        Wondering no more.

—*Carolyn Bahnck, fifth grade*

Mother Earth

As the woman fell to the hot sand,
She started to think about the child she once had,
About the husband she once had not so long ago,
And about the tribe she once had that she would roam the land, sea,
    and sky with.
As she sat there too dried out to drop a single tear for her tribe and
    her family,
She looked around at her only friends, the sun, the sky, the land, the
    plants.
And pleaded for forgiveness, and a child to look after.
Then something strange happened,
She felt a sharp pain, then the cry of a newborn baby
And she no more felt lonely but happy.

Then she looked around and silently said
Thank you to her friends,
She noticed that everything started to bloom and come to life,
And then a second baby was born,
But it was not a real person, it was an animal.
Then a bright light came down to her and told her, "You have been given the greatest
gift of all time, the gift to create life for all
kinds of living creatures."
Then she closed her eyes and started to think
of all her friends, opened her eyes and saw her
friends and family looking at her,
And from that day on she knew the earth
would have life on the land that she, once, roamed by herself.

  —*Melissa Janis, fifth grade*

Before, Before

I am the blue-green grass,
I bend into the water,
the quickly moving water is
angry,
angry with the vengeance of the
water-god,
He rushes by angrily,
He is mad at the people,
the people in the village,
they are hurting him with their
chemicals,
I have seen better days,
when the water-god was happy
gurgling and laughing,
before the people,
when animals came to drink,
before the hunters,
  Before, Before.

  —*Tania Philkill, sixth grade*

The flute calls to me.
Its sounds rush through my body
  As an eagle's feather
Falls at my feet.

A wolf calls
From the hills
  Joining the sweet sound
Of the music.

The fresh, warm air
From the desert
  Fills my lungs, as the flute
Seems to cease, but starts again.

This is a song of pureness and love.

  The flute calls to me
Its sounds rush through my body
  As I awake
From this dream of time.

  —Elisa Keller, seventh grade

The flute sounds like a boy lying on his bed.
        Looking at stars through his window.
  Trying to express his feelings by playing.
            He is sad, very hurt.
  He is thinking, wondering where everyone is.
      He is lonely, just him and his soul.
    He is calling for help, trying to see,
He is thinking, wondering if anyone's out there.
        Feeling the way he feels.

  —Danielle Scheel, seventh grade

Gone, but Still Alive

The medicine man comes through
  the opening in my teepee,
I lie under furs of animals
  I trapped last winter.
I lie now shivering from the disease.
  It is now part of me.
It grows with me, is me,
  and I am it.
We are one.
  The medicine man is becoming unclear,
as he kneels beside the fire
  to make my healing potion.
The medicine man starts dancing.
  I can feel his presence beside me.

By my head, my side, my feet,
    yet I cannot see him.
He is becoming more and more unclear.
    My shivering ceases.
All is black.
The medicine man is on earth,
but I am now in the sky.
    My soul is alive,
soaring above the medicine man.
    I am well, I am free!

    —*Katie Cleary, eighth grade*

The
soft wind
wakes up the
sleeping trees.
The cool green forest
is awakening to the radiant
dawn. The sun's golden rays
shine through the well-nourished
trees. The healthy animals scatter around
the forest bottom. The huge mountains stand
high above the never-ending sapphire sky. The forest
creatures scatter back to their homes. The sun goes down
like a ball of fire. The darkness of the sky blankets the
sleeping forest.

—*Brooke Holland, eighth grade*

As the culminating activity for a unit on history, social studies, or environmental science, writing poems while listening to "Earth Spirit" can help students organize new facts, reflect on their meaning, and make them their own. I have often asked students to think of *one* single thing, a fact or an idea that they remember from a recently completed unit, and to write a poem about what that fact or idea means to them. In this case, a judicious selection of poems read aloud at the beginning of the session, combined with the music, is all that is needed to get the poems started.

Sources

Joy Harjo, "Eagle Poem" and "Song for the Deer and Myself to Return On," from *In Mad Love and War* (Middletown, Ct.: Wesleyan Univ. Press, 1990).

Li Po, "Spring Night in Lo-Yang—Hearing a Flute," from *Chinese Lyricism* (New York: Columbia Univ. Press, 1971), translated by Burton Watson. Also available in *Talking to the Sun*, edited by Kenneth Koch and Kate Farrell (New York: Metropolitan Museum of Art/Henry Holt and Co., 1985).

Ramson Lomatewama, "An Evening at Windy Point for Christopher Jay," from *Ascending the Reed* (Flagstaff, Ariz.: Badger Claw Press, 1987).

R. Carlos Nakai's "Earth Spirit" flute music is available from Canyon Records Productions, 4143 N. Sixth St., Phoenix, AZ 85016.

Geof Hewitt

The Unplanned Collaboration

EVEN THE BEST writing assignments can grow stale. Initially, students respond well to almost any writing assignment I'm excited by. Their writing is fresh, the ideas and images are new, and everyone feels good about it. Remembering such assignments, which often arise spontaneously in response to what's going on in the classroom I'm visiting as writer-in-residence, I sometimes try them again with a new group of students. It's like telling a joke, though—the more often I tell it, the less laughter it provokes, even with a fresh audience each time.

But there is one writing assignment that never seems to fail me, and I use it as the opening exercise with almost any group of writers, regardless of age. In just seven minutes, each participant contributes to, and then becomes owner of, a rough draft—a healthy clump of words and images—from which to fashion his or her own piece of writing. At each step of the exercise, I am careful to keep the group's attention on the process, never revealing that I think the product of this effort will be the first draft of a collaborative poem.

After introducing myself to the group and explaining that my method of writing is to write as fast as possible, temporarily ignoring quality and accuracy during the process of composition, I abruptly introduce the dreaded moment: "Take out a pencil and a piece of paper." (It's amazing to me how many people are surprised, at the writing workshops I offer, that we are actually going to write!)

Because I am about to ask each person in the room to write a simple phrase, I sometimes review the definition of "phrase," depending on the sophistication of the participants. Then, as quickly and clearly as possible, I deliver the instructions: "Write a phrase—not a complete sentence, just a phrase—for some observation you experienced between waking this morning and arriving at this workshop. You have twenty-two seconds. Pencils up, get set . . . write!"

At the moment I call out "Write!" I apply my own pencil to the page, scrawling out whatever phrase I can. Of course, I do not watch the clock for a strict twenty-two seconds, but allow a little more time than it takes me to finish my phrase. Then, at random, I call on the participants to read their phrases, making sure they don't "tell" what they've written, but read directly from the page. (Often the "told" version is mushier and less direct than what is actually on the page.)

An option to calling on participants is to collect the written phrases, but I prefer having the phrases read to me as I write them on newsprint or the chalkboard, each phrase on its own line. I ask the participants to enter the same lines in their notebooks. Somewhere in the process I add my own phrase, and continue seeking contributions until everyone has responded or until I've used up the space on the newsprint or chalkboard. Typically, I manage to squeeze fourteen lines (a sonnet!) into the available space.

Here are phrases from a group of middle school students:

The springs on the seat are obliterated
Oatmeal again
Cloudy rainy atmosphere with colors all around
Beauty finds truth, truth finds beauty
A steaming hot egg sandwich
The sun radiating through the clouds
The wind was hauling
Run the car up on the sidewalk to park
I saw the leaves expressing themselves. Again.
Didn't know we had class
Dilettante's gaze
A sesame seed bagel that tasted like chicken broth
Cold wind
Freezing while waiting for the bus
Red ashy coals fading away in the windstove
The trees flew by like a blur as the sweat dripped off my brow

I write exactly what each student dictates, to the point of asking about punctuation and the spelling of homonyms (often an opportunity for laughter and a lesson on wordplay), always making sure the student reads exactly what he or she has written. When there's no more space on my writing surface, I read the responses aloud, carefully and slowly, using my voice to smooth over the rough spots, running the end of one phrase into the beginning of another to create unforeseen sentences. I present the piece as if it were a favorite poem, as if it is the well-polished final draft of a master. "Okay, what have we got here?" I ask.

Students will often respond, "A poem."

"All right, maybe so. But what makes it a poem?"

"It's all pretty much about the same thing—you know, morning images."

"Plus, the way you read it made it sound like a poem."

I make sure to mention that almost any piece of writing can be made to sound pretty good if it's read well. The reader's attention to speaking skills enhances the audience's response to a piece of writing. Even a diverse listing of images and phrases from different students— the equivalent of a bunch of random impulses from the individual writer's brain—can usually be made to sound like a unified piece. "Learn to read your work with assurance and pride," I say, "and you can sell cowflops for apple pies!" It might be argued that reading aloud becomes, in fact, a "revision" of the piece.

"Be sure you have copied these lines into your notebooks. I'm going to ask you to use this as your first draft and, for homework, to revise it into a poem or story that you've changed so much you can call it your own. Here are ways I might consider revising the piece." Then, spontaneously, I try to demonstrate as many strategies for revision as I can, announcing my biases as I go:

> The springs on the seat are obliterated,
> Oatmeal again! (*Exclamation point adds a little zip.*)
> Cloudy, rainy atmosphere with colors all around:
> Does beauty find truth, truth find beauty? (*Question mark adds variety, invites the reader's participation, but at the same time I announce my reluctance to use "truth" and "beauty" in a poem, saying I'll probably dump this line in a later draft.*)
> The sun radiates through the clouds (*Note the change to present tense; participles are really emasculated verbs—they've been robbed of tense!*)
> Like steam rising from my breakfast, my lame toe! (*Nonsense, perhaps, but a later revision may dump or save this expansion on the original response, with "lame toe" added because it is similar to "oatmeal," only spelled backwards—a little nod to wordplay. Later, we come to "sidewalk" and I point out that backwards, "sidewalk" is [phonetically] "clawed ice." Asked about "rising," I acknowledge that I'm letting a participle stand here, in spite of what I did to the previous line. Why? Because I'd have to change "like" to "as," resulting in "As steam rises," and that would cost me the simile created by "like.")*

The wind was hauling
as I ran the car up on the sidewalk to park.
I saw the leaves express themselves. Again. (*I really admire this use
of a fragment for emphasis. Omitting the ensuing three lines sacrifices some
excellent details, but seems necessary for continuity; maybe the lost lines
can be worked back into a later draft.*)
Cold wind knifed my jacket as I waited. (*Adding a verb and some
details for emphasis fills in the picture.*)
Trying to stay warm I thought of red coals
In the woodstove, then boarded the overheated bus: (*Adding
"overheated" justifies the poem's final image.*)
Trees blurred as sweat dripped off my brow.

"Needless to say, this was a fast revision, just to show you the kinds
of changes you might want to consider. I'll certainly go over the revisions I just made so hastily and reconsider each one because I know
that, although revision often leads to 'improvement,' it doesn't always
make things better!"

Here is another example of a first-draft collaborative poem, followed by two revisions. Here the assignment was for a group of high
school students to write a phrase, an observation from that very morning:

There are a lot more stoplights on Route 15 than there were in
    1968
House with a pond!
Sadie on top of the gravel pile
Damp blank closed sky
Rilla running around the room, "I'm naked Daddy!"
Beautiful mother and daughter.
A small bird sweeping towards my windshield.
A squirrel works an apple back up a tree.
Distance where I least expected it
Showerhead sprays in a circle
Fog—hanging on hillsides
"Bove and Fagan" on the ice cream truck
Everybody up down

Here is my on-the-spot revision:

Everybody Down Up

A lot more stoplights now on route 15
Than in 1968, but there's still that house with the pond!
And Sadie still sits on top of the gravel pile
In damp, blank, closed sky.

Inside that house I know Rilla runs around the room:
"I'm naked, Daddy!" Beautiful mother and daughter,
Small birds swoop my windshield
While a squirrel works an apple back up the tree.

Distance where I least expected it, once my home
I've got a motel where the showerhead sprays in a circle,
Fog hangs on hillsides and a "Bove and Fagan" ice cream truck
Is what my window looks out on and music plays, everybody up
     down.

Here is a version by writer and teacher Barry Lane:

Red Light 10 A.M. June 17, 1991

A small bird swoops
toward my windshield
Sadie at the top of
the gravel pile,
Damp
Blank
Closed
sky.
I think of
Rilla running
around the room,
last night,
"I'm naked Daddy!"
"I'm naked Daddy!"

Beautiful mother
     and daughter
this morning
at the breakfast table
eating
milk soaked
Cheerios

Outside,
A squirrel works an
     apple back
     up the tree.

Distance,
where I least
expected it.

Showerhead sprays
in a circle,
Fog hangs on
hillsides

More stoplights
on route 15
than there were in
1968

Barry published all three versions in his book *After THE END.*

Here are suggestions for students who may feel stuck in their approach to revision:

• Try to eliminate as many participles, adjectives, and adverbs as possible, strengthening as necessary the nouns and verbs they modify.

• Count the syllables in each line and create a "syllabic poem," in which the lines have the same number of syllables or another syllabic pattern.

• Rewrite the piece from the point of view and with the speech patterns of someone who is different from you: a supermarket checkout person, a five-year-old boy, the Queen of England, a ghost, etc.

• Review your piece to see whether the imagery is primarily visual, tactile, aural, olefactory, or cerebral. Create a second draft that either makes use of *all* the senses or focuses on just one. Note that the assignment was to write a phrase for an *observation*, not "something you saw." Nevertheless, a majority of responses are inevitably visual.

I recommend starting this exercise without a hint that the end product may be a poem because, all too often, when students think of "poetry," they conjure archaic romanticisms instead of immediate imagery, "truth finds beauty" versus "the wind was hauling." Further, a writer does not always know what a piece's form or genre will be until he or she has written a first draft.

In their revisions, some students will use only one or two of the lines of the original "poem," as a starting point or a central image. No matter how they accomplish these revisions, I give participants an opportunity to read and discuss their "final draft" responses.

What's important to me in this assignment is that students develop a broader awareness of poetic strategies, of the benefits of speaking distinctly and with feeling, and of a variety of approaches to revision. Maybe because this exercise covers all three of those bases and because it is group-oriented and fast, it is the only one that never fails me.

Janice Lowe

Painting Poems

> *I saw color and I saw a story. I saw a face and I knew a lifetime.*
> —Ntozake Shange, *Riding the Moon in Texas: Word Paintings*

ENCOURAGING TEENAGERS to get back in touch with the most imaginative sides of themselves isn't always an easy process. Too often, they've abandoned the sensory thinking of earlier youth for the kind of logical book report-oriented thinking that is rewarded in school. I try to show students that writing is an expression of one's individual perspective, a necessary fusion of inner and outer environments, a marriage of reality and fantasy. I tell them that what distinguishes and finally humanizes writing is the personal record of sensory and emotional detail. I, as reader, empathize with the familiar and am tantalized by the unknown, the quotidian as seen through another's eyes. The uniqueness of an individual writer's take on things is what draws me in. I tell young writers that they need to put themselves in their work and to take risks, no matter how they might feel.

One recent summer, I worked with mostly junior high school students at the Stapleton Branch Library on Staten Island. I'd worked there the previous spring with a group of students and because we'd had a good time together, I was expecting a fairly large number to return for the July workshop. Due to the whirlwind of summer activities including day camp, summer jobs, and, I was told vociferously by one librarian, the choice of blue Monday for one of the workshop days, we were fortunate to have the consistent attendance of four students.

One of the four was Diana Sheriff, an eight-year-old who, according to the proposal, could not possibly have participated in the workshop because she was not part of the young adult population served by the library. I enjoyed Diana's presence. She quickly became comfortable with getting right to the sensory, with using unusual word combinations to describe ordinary things—an impulse related to the invention of vocabulary, the formation of language. Her sister Makeda, age thirteen, and April Malone, age twelve, had attended the previous workshop and were already used to my coaching methods and warm-up activities: drawing or role-playing images in poems; experiencing poetry or music in a slightly darkened room. Although Diana was supposed to be amusing herself elsewhere in the library that first day, she seemed to be enjoying the relaxed feel of the workshop room. I asked her to stay and try her hand at writing. At first, Diana needed convincing that she could write. She worried a lot about spelling and was afraid of embarrassing herself in front of the older kids. In order to get her involved, to let her know that I valued her input, I suggested that the group write a collaborative sensory poem. Beginning with Diana and including the librarian Alberta Muir, the poets called out lines and I wrote them down:

> heat feels like
> hanging grapes out the window
> to turn to raisins
> like frying an egg on Dad's truck
> and getting into trouble
> like boiling water on the floor
> like ice cream melting

After checking out our sticky heat hot noise warm-up piece, we were ready to try Painting Poems, one of my favorite writing assignments.

In her book *Riding the Moon in Texas: Word Paintings*, Ntozake Shange creates a prose/poetry dialogue with works of visual art she feels connected to. In the prologue she writes, "I speak to these sculptures, wood prints and paintings as I would to a friend over coffee or champagne." She emphasizes that her conversation with art is not "an explanation of a visual maze," that writers can re-interpret and be creatively inspired by visual metaphors. I wanted similarly to inspire the poets of Stapleton Library.

In the next session, I gave each student a postcard of a William H. Johnson painting. The students seemed to relish observing "paintings" they could hold in their hands. I talked a bit about Johnson's life. He was an African-American artist who painted portraits and scenes in a murky impressionist style. He studied painting formally in Provincetown, Massachusetts, and in Europe, and didn't want to be restricted by a racist art world to painting in the black folk style that sometimes captured his imagination. Johnson's "folk paintings," however, were well-received in the States; it is for this work that he is best known.

These paintings are characterized by a sensual fluidity, startling and bright color combinations, and intense depictions of life in Afro-America: an outdoor baptism; men in a chain gang; a dancing couple; a lynching. I asked the students simply to observe the paintings—no writing yet.

Then I dimmed the lights and put on a cassette recording of music by Brazilian percussionist Nana Vasconcelos. I asked them to freewrite, to let their images interact freely with images in the painting, to allow the musical sounds, and the images, feelings, and colors suggested by those sounds, to blend into each other on the page.

Doing the assignment along with students, I checked my own Johnson print and uttered bugged-out responses: *orange mule prays to the virused soul of a bongo tree screaming "thief, murder!"* or *yellow skying juices my licorice mood*—in an effort to get students to bring out sound and color.

I walked around the room and addressed questions to the group as a whole, and sometimes to individual students after carefully reading their work: *Try putting some of your sensory experience of this poem into your piece. Does the change in lighting affect your mood or your writing? What does the music smell or taste like? What colors do you hear? Do animals or objects speak or dance?* Some students tuned me out and proceeded to do reportage on their paintings. For others, the questions became catalysts to exploration.

Using my variation of writer/teacher Julie Patton's free association exercise, I encouraged students to experiment with how the imagistic qualities of music can blend with the musical quality of words to enliven and deepen writing.* Inspired by Johnson's paintings, their poetic stories began to acquire layers of music and color, as in mixed-media creations. Sounds from Vasconcelos's music (shakers, singing, insistent drums) began to blend with images from Johnson's work: The exaggerated features of Johnson's huge-limbed folk moved to a music that even inhabited the trees. Eyes became handclaps. Blinking was noisy. Colors travelled spilling songs as they moved. I also asked students to incorporate the incidental noise of the library into their poems—the air conditioner's hum, children chattering, and the room's lighting, decor, and mood—if they related to what they were writing about.

---

* See Julie Patton's article, "Deep Song," in *Educating the Imagination, Volume 2* (New York: Teachers & Writers Collaborative, 1994).

Makeda and April chose to freewrite in lines. Makeda's poem was
a dialogue with Johnson's painting *Red Cross Handing Out Wool for Knitting*. Her writing was filled with music:

The Sounds of a Cry

The bandages of the American Red Cross
touch the warmth of a helpless flesh.
Hands and toes reach out to beats
of a drum like a heart listening to
the sounds of a crying tongue. Children
watch the dark lights of a body
in pale washed-out cloth
move to a dead stop. A rattle of
blue is wrapped over a summer-like
skin. Eyelids clap as others
look on. The fire in the name
American speaks. The trees stand
to a drunken beat heard away
in far off bands of clouded
blue not knowing where it's leading
to. Cheers of purple are heard way
out there leaving no traces
of how or where to reach. People
wait for other signs.

Makeda's syncretism of mood, room, painting, and music helps give
her piece a grounded surreality and an unusual depth resonating with
insight into the motivations of her human and personified characters.

April conversed with *Jitterbugs*, another work by Johnson, and was
inspired to write a traditional narrative about an adult situation:

Young Love

Two young lovers
spin each other around
a look in each other's
eyes. She wonders if they'll
be together for the rest
of life. Not a care in the
world. In their colorful
apartment of orange, blue,
beige, and a scuff-marked
green floor, boxes of furniture
stand and watch the couple
dance. The cracks in the ceiling

are like doorways to venture
through. He is nervous about
the wedding. How is he going to
pay for a ring? No need to
worry now, for that is in
the future.

April's poem opens with a gorgeous, surprising image. Then like
the dancing lovers, the story spins itself. Her short staccato lines and
clever linebreaks challenge me as reader; my eyes fall into a sort of
visual rhythm established from the beginning. Vasconcelos's music is
not referred to but is integral to the poem's structure. Color details
from the painting give the piece a solid sense of place: "apartment of
orange, blue, / beige, and a scuff-marked / green floor, boxes of furniture." How "cracks in the ceiling" can become "doorways to venture
/ through," a gateway to hard times ahead, is interesting to ponder.
These explorations of the sensory, both physical and emotional, give
breadth to an already engaging narrative.

The young writers loved going inside the paintings and being
privy to the secrets of imagined lives. Using Johnson, Vasconcelos,
and the aural/visual experience of the workshop room allowed students to express and underscore the range of emotion and experience
reflective of a young teen's life. Baby poems these are not.

Mark Statman

Poetic Theory and
the End of Science

GOOD LESSONS seem to have lives of their own. I start out with an idea or a poem I'm interested in. I bring it to the classroom, experiment, play, make mistakes, develop it, watch it grow, and finally, when it seems like I can't do any more with it, I let it go and look for something new. Once I feel I can't get any more out of the lesson, I get bored. And once I'm feeling that way, so, I know, will the kids.

But this process is good. Constantly looking for new ideas and poems keeps me fresh as a writer and a reader. It keeps the teachers with whom I collaborate (who are often the same from year to year) pleasantly surprised; they're getting a chance to read and think about something new, too.

Recently, we've had a good time with Gary Snyder's "Work to Do toward Town" (a poem so descriptive you can draw it as a picture on the board). Mayra Jimenez's untitled poem about a bird and train has led to poems about small and large sounds, about the sounds of the day and the sounds of the night. Homero Aridjis's "There's a silence in the rain" is another great poem about sound, except his works with the idea of its absence. And Margaret Walker's "My Grandmothers Were Strong" has helped me to get kids to think about people they love in simple, magical, and heroic ways. I'm not teaching any of these poems right now, although remembering them for this essay has gotten me thinking how they might be "reincarnated," the new approaches I could take to bring them back into the classroom.

The lesson I *am* most interested in right now investigates the difference between scientific and poetic theory. In a way, it's a variation on the old strategy of "inventing" or "lying," but with a Whole Language kind of twist because it brings in some ideas from science (and sometimes math and social studies).

I start this lesson by talking with the kids about nature. As they talk, I write their ideas on the board: wind, volcanoes, birds flying, planets orbiting, oceans, birth, time, leaves changing colors, fruit from flowers, rainbows. In no time, the board is filled with ideas.

Sometimes a student will bring up something that doesn't seem to be a part of nature. Desks. Cars. Disneyworld. Usually, with primary grade kids, I've found it most useful to suggest that the difference between what's natural and not natural is that what's natural is not made by people. Thus, a tree is natural, but a desk isn't. Yes, it comes from wood, but because it's fabricated, it's not really something we'd consider as a natural phenomenon.

With third graders and up, though, their thinking can be much more sophisticated and you can have some wonderful discussions around the idea of the not natural. Desks are not natural? Why? Because they're made by people. They don't occur in nature. But aren't people natural? Isn't making things natural? Birds, bees, and otters do it. Cars are made of steel and steel comes from the earth. If Disneyworld isn't natural, isn't it natural to have fun? And what about schools? Isn't it natural to learn? Aren't buildings natural, since they're made of steel, stone, and glass?

I've noticed that for younger kids, the joy is in figuring out the categories, nature versus not nature, making order out of the world. For older kids, the joy seems to be in destroying the categories, creating chaos out of what we discover to be, if not artificial, seemingly arbitrary orders.

Once we've finished all this brainstorming (although I never call it this because it reminds them of Writing Process, which most of them seem to dislike), I'll talk with them about science and scientific theory. I'll mention my brother, who is a scientist, and whose work involves trying to explain how and why things happen. Leaves change color because the weather starts to get cold and the sap needs to flow towards the trunk so that the tree doesn't freeze. As the sap moves away, the leaves start to die. Rainbows come from light reflecting off and refracting through water. During this discussion, I'll ask them to talk about some of the "why does X happen" questions they've been dealing with in their science class.

Then I'll bring up the question of why night comes. Usually, they'll know: because the earth spins. This often leads to a discussion of the earth's rotation around the sun and why seasons happen. I'll ask some students to play sun and earth, with one child playing the role of the stationary sun and the other orbiting and rotating around it. As the earth-child moves, I'll ask questions: when is it night where we are? When is it night in China? When is winter here? When is spring? I'll ask someone new to play the part of the moon, orbiting around the earth but never rotating. Why does the moon shine? (It reflects the light of the sun.) When is the moon full? When is it half? We'll perform a lunar eclipse, then a solar.

Then we'll talk about what the scientists do. Their job isn't just to think about what's happening in space. They also have to prove it. And they can't just prove it once. They have to prove it over and over to show that their explanation is correct and true one hundred percent of the time. Then I'll tell the kids about poetic theory. When it comes to explaining why things happen, poets, unlike scientists, can let their imaginations go crazy. They can invent and lie. They don't even have to be consistent. I'll write this on the board: scientific theory, the truth; poetic theory, craziness, inventing, lies! Then, I'll read them Victor Hernández Cruz's "Theory of Why the Night Comes":

The blue sky gets tired
The silver light of the moon
turns into a broom
And starts sweeping blue
sheets
Slowly the horizon changes
into a nightgown
and jumps over the moon
Into the mouth of the sun
Which takes it with it
To fry bamboo shoots
in China

After I read the poem I give everyone a copy. With younger kids, you may need to explain what bamboo shoots are. If the class doesn't get the poem right away, I'll ask the kids who have played sun, earth, and moon to come and act again, except now they have to act it the way Cruz's poem says it happens. The moon sweeps. The sun opens its mouth wide and catches the horizon nightgown (but, please, don't swallow). The earth turns and the sun spits the horizon out, while frying the bamboo shoots. The moon shines on the other side of the earth.

I have them do this play-acting several times. Then we'll do the scientific version one more time. Then the poetic. Which is true, I'll ask. The scientific one, they'll say. But which is more fun? The poetic one! Go, Victor!

Next, I'll ask them to come up with their own poetic theories. The board is still covered with their lists of natural phenomena, but I make sure they know they're not restricted to what's there. Anything in "nature" is fair game.

The Sun

The sun wakes us up
by blowing in our faces
and when I wake up
I tell him to leave me alone
and I'm still tired
and it makes the world
CRAZY

—*Tamara Allen, second grade*

The river is my water
because the river is water
and half is the soda
The volcanoes will be my lamp
and the ocean will be my juice
I go to break the lamp
and make apple juice

—*Anthony Vasquez, second grade*

Why Thunderstorms Come

The stars tease the sun about
how he is too big
The sun gets mad and turns off
his light
The sun roars at the stars and
flashes his anger with his light
The stars start to cry at their
stupidness

—*Toby Schneider, third grade*

The Universe

The universe is black
The planets spit out all
the black so they can be the

most beautiful
And at the end the
Universe is the ugliest
He is sad and all the
planets laugh

  —Ethan Silverstein, third grade

Weather Changes

Sun breaking through clouds
bright skies arrived

Rejoice in order
A new day forms

Rain falls sleek and messy
making puddles everywhere
yellow raincoats
yellow rain hats crowd the
streets

Our day comes to a stop

  —Tiffany Chambliss, fifth grade

Sunset

Look into the sky
gleaming sun blinding me
golden like blooming sunflowers
like fire burning
shining like a brand new pair of
shoes
it's a wonderful sight
turn my head
it's gone
burning fire
sun flowers
shine
 gone
   sunsct

  —Stephanie German, fifth grade

Sun and the Ocean

The sun is lemonade
The ocean is a ghost
The wind is snow
The volcano is orange
because it ate the sun

> —*Todd Rympalski, first grade*

Time

Time goes everywhere around
the world
If time was backwards
the morning is night
and night is morning
and we sleep in the future

> —*Jacob Cohen, first grade*

How the Night Comes

The flowers started to eat the
insects and flew to the stars
The animals started to eat the
sun
The people flew in space and ate
the clouds
The yellow solar system flooded
the ocean
The moon started to eat the
green blankets

> —*Christine Schwall, first grade*

Scientists, beware. The poets are coming to explain it all to you.

Sources

Homero Aridjis, in *Un ojo en el muro / An Eye through the Wall*, ed. Enrique R. Lamadrid and Mario Del Valle (Santa Fe, N.M.: Tooth of Time Books, 1986).

Victor Hernández Cruz, *Red Beans* (Minneapolis, Minn.: Coffee House, 1991).

Mayra Jimenez, *Cuando Poeta* (out of print).

Gary Snyder, *No Nature: New & Selected Poems* (New York: Pantheon, 1992).

Margaret Walker, in *Black Sisters: Poetry by Black American Women 1746–1980*, ed. Erlene Stetson (Bloomington, In.: Indiana Univ. Press, 1992).

Jack Collom

The Chant Poem

for Jerome Rothenberg

The tree.
The tree swayed.
The tree swayed with.
The tree swayed with a.
The tree swayed with a girl.
The tree swayed with a girl swinging.
The tree swayed with a girl swinging on.
The tree swayed with a girl swinging on one.
The tree swayed with a girl swinging on one of.
The tree swayed with a girl swinging on one of its.
The tree swayed with a girl swinging on one of its branches.
Its branches were.
Its branches were suffering.
Its branches were suffering because.
Its branches were suffering because the.
Its branches were suffering because the girl.
Its branches were suffering because the girl was.
Its branches were suffering because the girl was so.
Its branches were suffering because the girl was so heavy.

—Kristine Acquino, fifth grade

THE CHANT POEM is a form that catalyzes energetic and expansive student poems and yet offers numerous formal techniques, such as the use of repetition.

Chant poems draw on the ancient roots of poetry. Some qualities of poetry have been with us since the beginnings of talk. Poetry existed long before writing: just look at the amazing bodies of song and recital preliterate peoples have today. Anthropologists speculate that poetry—as distinct from speech—probably began in religious ceremonies, perhaps around a fire, to accompany dance. Nonsense syllables chanted rhythmically may have been the first poems. These vocalizations grew into song and poetry, which at base are the same.

In his book *Primitive Song*, C. M. Bowra gives some interesting ethnographical background:

> Song begins with some sort of tune, and to adapt real words to it is a separate and subsequent task which calls for considerable dexterity. . . . When Captain Charles Wilkes of the H.M.S. *Beagle* visited Tierra del Fuego in March 1838, the first inhabitants whom he met belonged to the Yamana. Two of his company visited them in their huts and received an unexpected greeting. Their mode of expressing friendship is by jumping up and down. They made Messrs Waldron and Drayton jump with them on the beach, before entering the hut, took hold of their arms facing them, and jumping two or three inches from the ground making them keep time to the following song:

> Ha ma la
> ha ma la
> ha ma la
> ha ma la
>
> O la la la la la
> la la la la

It's good to know that the music comes first; rhythm and sound have primacy over meaning. Knowing this encourages students to use abstract, "nonsense" words in their own poems.

As words with meanings got into the act, they too tended to be repeated a lot—for meaning, memory, and magic, as well as music— as in this tiny but poignant Bushman song:

> Famine it is
> Famine it is
> Famine it is here

Or in the Semang song about wild ginger:

> The stem bends as the leaves shoot up,
> The leaf-stems sway to and fro,
> To and fro they sway in various ways,
> We rub them and they lose all their stiffness,
> On Mount Inas they are blown about,
> On Mount Inas, which is our home,
> Blown about by the light breeze,
> Blown about is the fog, blown about is the haze,
> Blown about are the young shoots,
> Blown about is the haze of hills,
> Blown about by the light breeze,

It nods upon the hills,
It nods upon the hills of Inas,
Hills of Beching, hills of Siong,
Hills of Malau, hills of Kuwi,
Hills of Mantan, hills of Lumu,
Upon every mountain is our home.

This piece has a sort of overlapping structure that gives a feeling of an intimate geography of the Malaysian jungle.

Chanting and dancing are linked by their use of repetition. One example of this basic tie between dance and poem is the following Eskimo women's song from the Mackenzie River:

My arms they wave high in the air
My hands they flutter behind my back / they wave above my head
    like wings of a bird
Let me move my face / let me dance / let me shrug my shoulders /
Let me shake my body
Let me fold my arms / let me crouch down
Let me hold my hands under my chin

Repetition establishes rhythm and enchants the listener. But *only* to repeat gets boring, hence variety. Repetition and variety are opposites that co-exist and strengthen each other.

Alliteration and rhyme in "primitive" chant poetry occur richly but intermittently. The music is ever-shifting, just as it is in that most modern Western phenomenon, free verse. The best chant poems are expansive: each stage is lovingly lingered in, at the level of word, line, stanza, and then developed by a sequence of images.

Chant poems are fine for people of all ages to write. Within the form's flexible constraints, any degree of sophistication or simplicity can operate. A good approach is to write the words *repeating* and *changing* on the board and let students know that these are the keys. Read some examples by adults and kids, energetically emphasizing rhythm. Aim for variety, and show the students how the different examples work, exactly how they repeat and change. With older students you can use a sophisticated example such as D. H. Lawrence's "Bavarian Gentians" (which has eighteen uses of the word *dark*, including nine in the second eight-line stanza alone).

Next, ask your students to pick their own word, phrase, or idea, write it down, and start playing with it on paper, making up ways of "keeping it in the air." Simply giving a range of options and encouraging inventiveness can evoke wonderful spontaneous pieces from the kids. I discovered over the years that it helps to discourage the formulaic; specifically inveigh against the tedious In-the-kitchen-there's-a-knife / fork / spoon / pot / pan / eggbeater / wall / floor / mom sort of regularity. Of course, repetition is important, but so is chaos and wildness; the repetition helps prevent the chaos from slipping into entropy. Above all, urge *invention*. It's best to have students concentrate on writing one poem each. Chant poems are usually best fairly long, to give the rhythms some room to develop. If students have trouble getting started, have them write down a word, take a deep breath, and just start improvising on paper. Remind them that they can always scratch it out and begin again. If a student feels his or her poem is done, you can suggest a "Part II," taking off on a new tack.

Then collect the students' poems and read them aloud—or better still, have the students read them. If they do, emphasize performance values and rhythm.

Below are some good example poems by adults and children, with commentary.

Walt Whitman rolled out his long lines with a great deal of chant sensibility, as in the following excerpt:

Ever the hard unsunk ground,
Ever the eaters and drinkers, ever the upward and the downward
    sun,
Ever myself and my neighbors, refreshing, wicked, real,
Ever the old inexplicable query, ever that thorned thumb, that
    breath of itches and thirst,
Ever the vexer's hoot! hoot! till we find where the sly one hides and
    bring him forth,
Ever the sobbing liquid of life,
Ever the bandage under the chin, ever the trestles of death.

Closer to the contemporary are these excerpts from Anne Waldman's "Fast Speaking Woman":

because I don't have spit
because I don't have rubbish
because I don't have dust
because I don't have that which is in air
because I am air
let me try you with my magic power:

I'm a shouting woman
I'm a speech woman
I'm an atmosphere woman
I'm an airtight woman
I'm a flesh woman
I'm a flexible woman
I'm a high-heeled woman
I'm a high style woman . . .
I'M A SILVER LIGHT WOMAN
I'M AN AMBER LIGHT WOMAN
I'M AN EMERALD LIGHT WOMAN . . .
   I'm the rippling woman
   I'm the gutted woman
   I'm the woman with wounds
   I'm the woman with shins
   I'm the bruised woman
   I'm the eroding woman
   I'm the suspended woman
   I'm the woman alluring
   I'm the architect woman
   I'm the trout woman
   I'm the tungsten woman
   I'm the woman with the keys
   I'm the woman with the glue

   I'm a fast speaking woman

      water that cleans
      flowers that clean
      water that cleans as I go . . .

Kids don't usually get self-conscious about a *lot* of repetition—which makes them naturals at chant poems:

People look People
people how people
people many people
people times people
people I people
people told people
people this people
people stupid people
people person people
people to people
people say people
people people people

   —*Eylin Velez, eighth grade*

(Read this poem down as well as across.) Rhythm flourishes here due to double *p*'s (percussive pop) in *people*.

> When I look into the light I see dancing girls doing a marathon
>   dance.
> When I look into the light I see brightness & darkness.
> When I look into the light I see the gentle fast movement of the light.
> When I look into the light I see the electricity passing through the
>   lines to the light.
> When I look into the light I see a crispy sharp look.
> When I look into the light I see the nice blue waters moving to a
>   rhythmic beat.
> When I look into the light I see the light is talking to me.
> When I look into the light it's telling me, "Look, smell the rhythm."
> When I look into the light it smells delicious & sweet, innocent &
>   harmless.
>
> *—Anonymous, fifth grade*

In this poem, a large, primal vision develops out of an everyday optical fact. The poem's scatteredness helps offset the extreme regularity of the line beginnings.

> The tune
> The tune
> The tune
> The tune
> Never miss
> The tune
> The tune
> The tune
> The tune
> Cause you never miss
> The tune
> The tune
> The tune
> The tune
> Cause THE TUNE IS COOL!!
> AND YOU NEVER NEVER Want
> to get rid of the? . . .
> tune
> The tune
> The tune
> The tune Yaaaa!!
>
> *—Grace Kruszewski, third grade*

Poetry is falling down
Poetry is letters
Poetry is 1-2-3
Poetry falls off the waterfall and hits its head
Poetry is sliding off a rainbow
Poetry is like a lion climbing up a rainbow
Poetry is like a kite
Poetry is like the air
Poetry is like the air in the sky
Poetry is like white clouds
Poetry eats horses
Poetry is like the spring
Poetry is like summer
Poetry is like a candle burning out all by itself
Poetry is climbing up the mountain like a cloud
Poetry is the sky all over the world
Poetry is like a cry
Poetry is like a fluffy pillow
If you don't wear a helmet you might get hit in the face
Poetry is like a radio walking into the zoo
Poetry is funny
Poetry is like someone eating ice cream
Poetry is like a bow on its head
Poetry looks like ice cream
Poetry is like a blue butterfly in the sky
Poetry is like somebody eating a peanut
Poetry touches the lightbulb and pulls the string and falls down

   —*Class collaboration, kindergarten*

On this occasion I served as chalkboard secretary for the lines
the kids called out.

I hate
hate strange
strange people
people only
only smoke
smoke little
little lines
lines white
white shades
shades darken
darken shores
shores swish
swish bowl

bowl burning
burning furiously
furiously I

—*Lola Benjamin, twelfth grade*

Lola's poem is tough, slim, original.

Cats go crazy
Cats go crazy like
Cats go crazy like me
Cats like
Cats like to
Cats like to go
Cats like to go crazy
Cats like to go
Cats like to go downtown
Cats like to
Cats like to drive
Cats like to drive cars
Cats like to drive a car but bang boom crash
Cats like to
Cats like to wreck
Cats like to wreck into
Cats like to wreck into you
Cats like people
Cats like people to
Cats like people to scratch
Cats like kids
Cats like kids to
Cats like kids to play
Cats like kids to play with
Cats are dead because they got in so many wrecks

—*Crystal Jensen, fourth grade*

The following poem ends with a reference to the teacher, whose name is Meridean.

Two-timer elephants using some
kind of elephant ventriloquism
elephant pies plus elephant cakes
calling 200,000 elephants reading
awesome elephant poetry
like elephant ice cream cones
tax-collector elephants shot by

poachers looking for elephant
ivory always around for
elephant mischief contracting
rats trying to do elephant
multiplication and elephants
step on other rodents eating
the elephants' acorns ironic
supersonic elephants charging
at some elephant book of poetry
iguanas eating elephant hide
watching some dramatic elephants
reading iguana poetry leaving
elevated elephants who are
anti-iguana carnivore elephants
eating other elephants wearing
3-D sunglasses made especially
for elephants who are waking
at dusk while the Greenwich
Prime Meridean is facing the sun.

—*Benjamin Miller, fifth grade*

Sources

C. M. Bowra, *Primitive Song* (New York: New American Library, 1963).

Anne Waldman, *Fast Speaking Woman* (San Francisco: City Lights, 1975).

Walt Whitman, *Leaves of Grass* (many editions).

Mark Grant Waren

What You Always
Wanted to Say To...

I'M A PLAYWRIGHT. In the past five years, I have taught playwriting and collaborative script development (using improvisation and theater games) in a wide variety of residency programs. I've taught inner-city kids and rural mountain kids, and I'm always surprised by how many issues seemingly disparate groups of students have in common.

Likewise, I'm always surprised by how often it's the honors students who have the most difficulty "giving up" their hard-earned essay-writing skills for the very different techniques involved in dramatic writing. I've worked in schools where the star playwrights were kids who had been classified as "learning disabled" by their school administrations.

I usually don't find it hard to get students writing plays. Of course, first you need to develop a warm, supportive, constructive atmosphere in the classroom, and to surmount students' initial fears of a new form. Once they try it, however, their interest quickly grows. Playwriting is closer to speech than are other genres. I tell my students: "Forget about paragraphs, forget about writing in complete, grammatical sentences. Do you talk to your friends in complete, grammatical sentences? If a person talks that way in a play, that *says something* about who that character is, where he or she comes from, what activities he or she performs in life. Who do you know who talks in complete, grammatical sentences?"

They answer, "Teachers." "Principals." "You." And sometimes, "My parents."

I begin my playwriting residencies with monologues, to accustom students to listening for a single voice. Usually, I ask students to write monologues based on a family member, a good friend, or some other close acquaintance. Students already know these voices: a mother on the telephone with a friend, a sibling bragging about his or her performance in a basketball game, a grandparent telling a story of days long past. Students know the voice of a friend telling what happened at the party they weren't allowed to attend, a teacher lecturing a class on its behavior, or a football coach getting the team psyched for the big game.

A typical first-draft family monologue is this moving one by a seventh grader from Mitchell County, North Carolina:

Grandfather

When I was very young, my mom died. This left me and my sister alone. My dad run off with another woman. I never seen my father. Some people came and took my sister Joyce away. They took me, but I ran away two weeks after that. I left State Louisiana and worked my way to North Carolina. I was only thirteen when I left, but I did not care. I knowed my dad was somewhere in North Carolina and I was going to find him. By the time I got North Carolina it was the middle of December. There were about a foot and half of snow on the ground. I went to my uncle house in Yancey County. When I got to his house, it was the middle of the night. I beat on the door. When he come to the door, he asked me how I got to his house. I told him. He told me that my dad lived in Double Island. The next day, he took me to see my dad. I told what had happened. He went back to Louisiana and got my sister. Me and my sister stayed with him for eight years, till I went into the army.

Note that although a distinctive character voice is emerging, there is no clear dramatic context for this monologue. We do not know to whom the grandfather is speaking, or why. For me, this is the reason the monologue runs out of steam at the end: the student still hasn't *pictured* his grandfather telling this "story" in a dramatic context.

Compare "Grandfather" with this dramatically realized "phone monologue" by a high school junior in Roxboro, North Carolina:

Cousin Jennifer

JENNIFER (*on phone*): Yes, Mommy, I won't do that again. Yes, Mommy . . . Yes, Mommy . . . Yes, I finished the dishes. Yes, I ate breakfast. No, it was not junk food. I ate eggs. Yes, I'll finish the floor. Joanie will help me. Yes, the room is clean. I won't go outside . . . I won't bring my friends into your clean kitchen. Yes, I can clean up after myself. I'm not lying. I didn't do that. I swear, Mommy. But . . . I'm not lying. I didn't do that. I think Joanie did it. I'm not blaming her for something I did. She did it. Okay, I'll tell her. Yes, Mommy. Yes. She's right here. Would you like to speak to her? Yes. I love you, Mommy. Here she is.

Or with this powerful monologue by a high school senior, also from Roxboro:

Kate

The setting is a dimly lit hospital room. An unconscious young woman lies on a bed with life-sustaining equipment attached to her. A tired-looking woman, about forty, enters.

KATE (*softly stroking her pale daughter's palm-up hand, she moves a finger up the girl's arm.* KATE *stops and lovingly stares at a small white scar just below the girl's elbow*): Hmm, you always did have a way with glass. I remember the day you made this little imperfection. You were about four years old and always into something. We had that ranch house in Florida, you were so happy then. You bounded up the steps with your new discovery, a tiny, helpless lizard trapped in a bright green Sprite bottle. You were so proud, you came just a-running to tell me. When you fell and broke the bottle, you were more concerned about the escaping lizard than cutting your arm. You were so brave, so much trust, so much faith in your mom. You came home and showed everyone your stitches, and then your scar.

But now, you have new scars to tell about, don't you. Oh, God, dear God, please, please, don't take her from me. She's all I have left. Please.

Life is funny, you know? Who would have thought that the sweet little baby I held in my arms, not so long ago, would lose faith in her mom, so soon, and so easily. I know I've made mistakes, but I love you. I truly love you.

KATE stands frozen by her daughter's side. Curtain.

The authors of "Cousin Jennifer" and "Kate" have vividly imagined their monologues in a plausible stage setting. Note that even though some of Kate's sentences are awkward, we accept them in the dramatic context in which they occur. Good stage writing is not always "good writing" in the usual sense of the term. I tell my students, "Plays aren't meant to be read at home. They're meant to be performed. What you're writing is a set of instructions for an actor. There are two types of instruction in a play: *Say this* (the dialogue) and *Do this* (the stage directions)."

There are many roads that lead to good dramatic writing. "Kate" and "Cousin Jennifer" both involve a selective reconstruction of a character's "real" speech rhythms under specific dramatic pressures (the mother's phone call, the sick daughter). Equally enjoyable in a different way is this wholly fantastical voice one eighth grader invented for his cat:

> Listen, I know you're mad at me, but hey, it wasn't my fault. You never should have left the fish on the countertop. I was hungry, and being a cat, I hopped up and ate it. You might as well have poisoned me. You know I hate halibut. Yech! Well, I've learned my lesson. Can I have my Alpo back now? Please! You should've known not to set fish out with me around. Ever since you fed me that flounder left over from supper when I was a kitten, you've known that's the one thing I go crazy for (catnip too!). Besides, I'm just a gourmet food tester. Why, I can't even see why you would buy halibut. (Humans, you rub around their leg and they'll forgive anything!) Yeah, come over here and pet me. Oh, no! You saw! I'm really really sorry, see I was aiming at the litter box and here comes that stupid dog of yours. By the way, have you ever thought about having him fixed? I know a great veterinarian. What, me change the subject? Who ever heard of such a thing? I'm just your nice kitty. Yeah. I'll purr. They love it when I do that. Could you do me a favor? My collar's a little tight. Yes, much much better. While you're at it, you might want to scratch my belly when I roll over. Bath? No, not me, I don't . . . Please! Nooooo!! [*sound of splash*] RARRRRR MEEOOOWW HISSSS . . . Come back here, you little . . . You soaked me! When I catch you, I'll. . . . Don't blame me. I didn't do it!

Dramatic writing is never "finished." It is always subject to revision in performance. In rehearsal, the author of "Kate" (who also played the title role) found that she needed to introduce additional pauses and that these pauses heightened the effect of her character's words. I tell my students that they need to imagine their play on stage as concretely as they imagine the reality or fantasy they wish to portray on stage.

Students usually respond well to playwriting. Occasionally, however, depending on the time of day, the phase of the moon, the oppressiveness of the school environment, etc., we hit an impasse. When the cats aren't hissing and the families aren't fighting and even the grandparents have stopped telling stories, I pull out my tried and true "Old Faithful" playwriting exercise, which I call, "What You Always Wanted to Say To. . . ."

This exercise is the Jiffy Lube of playwriting exercises, guaranteed to start every one of your students writing within three minutes. (Yes, even the three stoners in the back row, the table full of girls so shy they never read their pieces aloud, the football players, and even the student who thinks you're prejudiced against him or her and has been favoring you with looks that could kill.)

I never include this exercise in my regular plan. This one is for emergencies only. All it requires is being able to switch gears quickly and to deliver the following speech with conviction.

"Okay, we seem to be stuck here. Does everyone agree?"

They all agree.

"Let's try something completely different. You're going to write a monologue in *your own* voice. You're the person speaking the monologue.

"Here's the situation. The scene is your living room. On the sofa is a member of your family. It could be your mother, your father, your brother, your sister—whoever. There's a magic force field around this person, so they can't move, and they can't talk back. This is your chance to tell them what you always wanted to say to them, but never could. Anything you want. You could be telling them what a rotten, stupid person they are and how much you hate them. You could be telling them how wonderful they are and how much you love them. You have to choose someone to whom you have at least a half a page of things to say. Important things. Things that have been dying to come out. You have fifteen minutes. Does anyone have any questions? Does everyone have paper and pencil? I'm going to do this one too. Okay, go."

Unless you have a class that needs a lot of help, so that you have to circulate, I urge you to do the exercise along with the students. That way you get to share in the writing community, and your students see and hear you taking the same risks you are asking them to take.

While you don't have to memorize my speech, it *is* important to present the exercise quickly and with enthusiasm, as a real break from what you've been doing. You also don't have to stick to family members. With a high school class you could give them the option of monologizing to buddies, boyfriends, girlfriends, or even teachers and school officials. (If you do this, you won't believe the results you get, but I wouldn't try that unless you really are prepared to hear *anything*!) If you're willing to listen, however, you may learn some important things—and not just from monologues that are addressed to you.

This assignment works well because it frees students from the constraints of form and lets them focus instead on expressing their feelings. The form is ready-made. The exercise breaks down walls between students, between students and teacher, and between students and playwriting. We can *tell* students that playwriting is a form of expression, but it helps for them to actually *feel* that as a raw reality.

I have done this exercise with public school students from fourth grade to twelfth, as well as with professional playwrights and teachers in staff development workshops. The results are surprising, often funny or moving, sometimes (less often than you might think) scatological or abusive. The following excerpt is from a monologue by a high school sophomore:

> [*To a mother*] Please respect my choices, even if they're different than yours. Don't automatically assume that I'm doing everything just to annoy you. I have a brain, and I can think, and I'm not just being negative. I really think about things. . . .

A high school freshman in Person County, North Carolina, wrote this monologue to an uncle only a few years older than the author:

> Man, don't you know that stuff's killing you? You've changed, man, you don't hang out with the fellas anymore. You don't have fun anymore, and your mother's worried. You need to get help, man, before you mess up your life for good. Think what you have to live for. You have a wife, two kids, a nice house, and you're willing to throw it all away for drugs, just to get high. Man, it's not worth it. Get help. You'll thank yourself in the long run. Especially when you see your daughter graduate high school, maybe even college, become successful and spoil your grandchildren when you're old and funky. Just think, you could get some bad rock and die tomorrow. You have so much to live for. Get help.

Sometimes, the monologues rehearse statements of independence, like this one by a high school junior:

> I am sorry, Mother, but I cannot follow your prejudiced ways. I am my own person and will live my life the way I think is best. Mother! I am nothing like you, only by blood. You think you can run my life, but you cannot. I refuse to reject my friends because they do not live up to your standards. Your ignorance of the situation will only lead to the bitter hatred I feel towards you at this moment. I have learned to respect people for the goodness in them, instead of their differences. I will live my life and you will live yours. So, goodbye, Mother. I am leaving home.

Note that in the two preceding monologues, there is not only a clear speaker, but a clear person being addressed and a clear dramatic reason for speaking at that moment. It is important to point out these positive qualities to students, so that they can bring them to their future dramatic writings.

I always try to allow enough time for at least four students to read their pieces in a class period. I tell students: "We are a writing community. When we criticize, we criticize to help someone make their writing better, not to diss it. So we always start by saying what we like about the monologue, what was strong about the writing. Then we ask: 'Was the voice of the speaker consistent?' (*Not*: 'Was it real?') 'Was the scene clear and complete? What could be improved? Where else could the playwright go with this monologue—a longer work, a revision, an expansion?'"

What are the pitfalls of this exercise? Common questions students ask beforehand are: "Will we get in trouble for this?" "Can we use cusswords?" "Do we have to hand these in?" You'll need to decide what you're comfortable with. You may want to have the whole class agree that these pieces won't be discussed outside of the classroom, and that no one write a monologue addressed to someone who is actually part of the class. And while some of the examples I have quoted would be welcome anywhere, some of the angrier pieces may not find a place in your student's portfolio. That's too bad, because especially with some particularly alienated students, their angry work may contain some of their best writing.

If you are not shy of controversy, you may find that this exercise opens the door to many fruitful conversations and debates that might not otherwise have occurred. After the reading of a shy African-American high school junior's vitriolic denunciation of a junior high school teacher in another district, whom he considered racist, the class had an extraordinary discussion about their experiences of prejudice in the schools and their communities. Students formed lasting bonds of understanding across racial lines. Like all good theater, this exercise tends to expose what is hidden. Theater (even classroom theater) is always a rehearsal for life.

I call this type of monologue the External Monologue, since it's a speech directed at another character (either present on stage or not). Two other monologue forms are the Internal Monologue, or Soliloquy, and the Direct Address Monologue, in which a character consciously addresses the audience (as, for example, in Chekhov's "The Harmfulness of Tobacco"). In general, I avoid Direct Address Monologues with students, because they already have a tendency to lecture, but there is an interesting variant on "What You Always

Wanted to Say To . . . ," using the Internal Monologue, the "To Be or Not to Be" exercise.

Start by reading your students some sample soliloquys, including the famous one from *Hamlet.* Then ask them to recall a critical moment of decision in their lives, or to imagine a future moment of decision. It's important that they be faced with a decision in the situation, even if they do not end up making a clear choice. Then ask them to write what they said to themselves—or what they imagine themselves saying. Give them a time limit, and allow time for reading and discussion.

I mentioned earlier that whenever possible you should do this exercise along with your students. In doing so, you make yourself a part of the writing community, putting yourself on the line with your students, who will be fascinated by your participation. Don't give yourself the spotlight, but also don't hesitate to read your piece if your students ask. With a shy class, you can lead—"I'll read mine first." Here's one I wrote to my father, who is still alive, a retired director and theater scholar:

> Yeah, Dad, I love you. That's always been very hard for me to say. It took you thirty years to return a hug from me, and it's taken me thirty years not to think of you as an enemy. That's too long. We can do better with each other. I understand you better now—why you were so distant, what happened to you as a child. . . . The one thing I wish is that we could have shared more together. When you directed my play, that was like a dream to me. Do you know how long I had wanted to work with you? I remember as a teenager, asking Mom if I could go to one of your classes, and the answer always being some vague "no." I grew up in your theaters, but you never shared what you were doing with me. Your work was always over there, and I was here, and you mainly lived over there. Then later, when you did try to talk, I couldn't listen, because I was so angry. I hated you. Even now, sometimes. . . . There's so much we could have learned from each other—so much we still can learn. Would you teach me things? I can listen now. I can learn. From you.

Madeline Tiger

The Name Game

ONE'S OWN NAME is the key to a store of powerful emotions, admitted or not. Everyone is excited by his or her name—by its sound and look, its history and legendary connotations, from family traditions to literary references. One is alert to its forms and versions, ways of saying it, ways of writing it. People "play with" their names and the names of people they care about; in doodles they design and repeat and decorate their names even when they are thinking or talking about other things—on the phone, at a meeting, in the classroom. The psyche reaches for something engaging; one's name proposes itself from within, the absolutely personal, the first word.*

We savor names. Just think of parents naming their children, how we enjoy the way a baby learns his or her name, and how we use nicknames. We have histories of changing feelings about our various names. We hear messages in our "given" names. "Maiden" names used to disappear; now they reappear. Middle names often have peculiar lives: many are withdrawn, but some go in front for a time. Names signify culture, tradition, religious rites, gender, family, language, and sometimes even one's generation. From the first small step in mastering the art of writing, we take special pains with our names. We take pride, sometimes amusement, and even comfort in signing our names. Adolescents are most obvious about it, but people of all ages love to write their names, even when the familiar act becomes automatic. Students are surprised when they see their names in new ways and excited when they find that they can make something new out of such stuff, one's own simple manuscript. The signature becomes an emblem of the self.

---

* I think I invented this lesson because I've always been self-conscious about my name, ever since I first went to day camp on a bus and the children teased me about being so little with such a fierce name. I told my father, and he taught me to growl! A number of years ago somebody encouraged me to learn more about my first name and I have been on a long pilgrimage into the Magdalen story ever since. I have shaped many poems out of what this rich and mysterious name has discovered for me.

The Name Game is simple. It promotes writing freely—and with courage. I most often use it as the first session with K–4 students, but it works well in all grades. I've used it in teachers' workshops, in training sessions for writers-in-the-schools colleagues, and in other workshops with adults. It is also effective with senior citizens' groups, especially in the introductory session.

First I make sure everyone has a piece of blank paper. I give small children large drawing paper, older children anything available. With adults I use regular unlined 8 $\frac{1}{2}$ x 11" sheets that have the following assignment written across the top:

THE NAME GAME

How the sound of a word changes . . . the different sounds of talking . . . the sound of asking a question or of answering . . . the sound of telling a secret.
    — Kenneth Koch & Kate Farrell, on Gertrude Stein

1. Write your name in the blank space below. Write it several times. Write your whole name or part of it. Use your nickname if you want to. Keep writing your name in whatever ways feel good to you. Repeat isolated parts or syllables if you like, or the whole name. Skip spaces, move the words around on the page, repeat different parts of the name . . . invent a pattern. Or see what pattern begins to emerge. Has anything new begun to appear? Have you discovered anything in your name?

2. Soon we will read these pages out loud and see what they sound like. Have you edited it in a special way? Is it still the same configuration, or is it a new architecture? When you sound it out, how does it feel? Poetry comes from naming, and from the sound of words, the look of words, and the way words interplay.

I give these written instructions only to adults or mature high school students. Giving a sheet with instructions and a blank area is a particularly efficient way of doing the exercise quickly.

In most situations, however, I spend some time introducing the exercise before the students write. I always pitch the lesson according to the age and style of the group. "What's the first word you ever learned to write?" I ask younger students, sometimes the older ones too. "What word belongs to you?" (They get it.) "Who here has ever been teased about your name? Whose grandmother calls you something funny? What does your mother call you when she's angry at you? Who knows where you got your first name or your middle name?" They become amused and excited and begin to talk to me and to each other.

We discuss tones—the way someone shifts the sound higher or lower or emphasizes a syllable in his or her name, to call one tenderly or angrily, to wheedle or scold, saying a name from far away (a parent calling from a window, a friend yelling up the street) or up very close (a grandmother cuddling a child, two lovers). We talk about the variants and uses of one's name, about how nobody should "call you out of your name"(insult someone by making fun of his or her name), and nobody should be entitled to change the spelling or make fun of your name—except you. We are asserting something about private space when we talk about ownership of names, and we are discovering that everybody in the room has something important to use in the writing.

If I sense that it's appropriate to discuss the social significance of different names, I may focus on the value of all kinds of names, of human styles and histories, of ethos and race, family and personal history. Children often appreciate a chance to share this information. Sometimes students go on to find out, from their parents and grandparents, more about the roots of their names, which can lead into further writing exercises. Furthermore—and this is very important—the process helps us to learn each other's names with care and with new awareness.

Time for the introductory conversation is completely elastic: the Name Game works whether or not you spend a long time talking about names.

For primary students, the act of writing something important is the main point of the lesson. Every letter is an emblem of creativity;

the name is shaped over and over, and the shaping is itself a stimulation. For older students the value is more complex: they benefit from both linguistic and cultural awareness, but also from the renewed permission to play. If a student seems embarrassed, I try to point out interesting features of his or her name.

When I give oral instructions, I tell students, "Hold the paper any way you want, turn it sideways or at an angle. Write up and down, around, or on a slant. You can even write backwards." (I don't usually mention this, they discover it). "Make it beautiful or funny or weird, delicate or strong looking. Fill up the page or leave some interesting spaces." I keep telling them how essential their names are, each one a clue to the self; and I emphasize their personal authority in using their names.

With teachers and other adult groups, after I give out the assignment sheet, I repeat the rules and insist that they must keep writing. (That's the hardest part to get teachers to do.) Sometimes I have young students use colored markers or crayons, and I encourage them to make pictures out of their letters, or to write their names and decorate them. Some students invent ways of hiding the letters in the design, unconsciously asserting their cabalistic tendencies: they are practicing the art of using language to hold secrets. The name is a symbol and a revelation, but it is also, paradoxically, a hiding place, a façade, something the owners can manipulate to suit themselves, like any piece of fictive writing, any work of art.

Children who say they hate their names provide a special challenge. Individually, I help them play with the letters and the sounds: I break apart the letters and help them discover delicious or funny or lovely words in their names. Sometimes I encourage them to do anagrams, but often I prefer to focus on the name in its original form, to find ways of honoring its look and its sounds, the rhythm of first, middle, and last names together, cute abbreviations—whatever I think of to help that student enjoy his or her name and feel proud of it.

As the writers begin to experiment with repetitions and splicings, new combinations, spacing, and initials, the resulting letters and phonemes become designs: some are elongated gracefully, some are very small, making rhythmic patterns.

You can feel the atmosphere in the room relax. The students breathe easier. You can see them peeking at each other's productions, amused by each other's designs. This is especially striking with teachers in a faculty workshop, when they catch onto the idea that all they have to do is play. Often they are so pleased by this release of work-as-play and by the seeming ease of the lesson that they keep the handout copy to try it in their classrooms soon. I urge them to share their own efforts with their students.

The pages fill. Even very young writers discover their power to use the space in interesting ways, with simple repetitions, then with variations, often ingenious. They love discovering other words inside their names (as with my own name: *Madeline made line(s) mad ma* and *deli*). They find humor in breaking up words, making staccato and obligato, reversing words or writing backwards—not only to create sound effects, but also because these maneuvers break convention. The first injunctions they have learned, "Spell your name correctly" and "Write it neatly," are suspended. Instead they hear, "Your name is yours, private, to do with as you wish, and nobody else can change it or make fun of it. But you can!"

This message has become increasingly important with the influx of children from many different cultures and language groups. Sometimes their names are hard for local children to learn; sometimes social pressures force newcomers to abandon their original names. The euphemism for this is "cultural adjustment," supposedly making multiculturalism easier. But all kinds of names are beautiful and interesting, as sounds, images, and symbols. The classroom must honor everybody's name.

After ten to twenty minutes of writing, I ask the students to share their work. In teachers' workshops there is usually amusement, at first nervous, then admiring. Young students work very hard, take the game seriously. They want to project their names with strength, flourish, or style, and they like to show off how many ways they can write.

I hold some of the students' pieces up, remark on their originality, on the use of spaces, patterns, lines, circles, and other shapes, and praise those papers that are completely filled. I also praise the spare designs that lead the eye up and down the page or into its corners. I ask students what kind of classroom this sounds like now, in what subject area do they discuss things this way, talking about line and shape and space? Art, they tell me. Yes. And poetry writing is also a visual art, I tell them. A poem has a shape, it has lines that take the eye here or there, it leaves spaces where the writer wants space. It can have very short lines or long ones, it can be vertical or horizontal, spread out or tightly contained.

Older students may act blasé when they are actually quite impressed by the variety and complexity of design in the room, but when I give the word, they show each other their work. Excited, sometimes they begin to read parts aloud to each other, mutually intrigued and impressed. I hear rhythms of many names in many voices rising around the room. This communication reinforces a sense of community.

Then I ask for volunteers to read their pieces to the whole class. I try to get each one to recite just what is on his or her paper, reading from top to bottom, side to side, or in any direction the design takes. We have to quell the urge to insert explanations of how one decided which of his or her names to use, how a name was divided, how the design was formatted, etc. And we have to hold back the telling of biographical anecdotes that lie behind the names. This becomes a lesson in economy of presentation, getting down to the poem.

If no one comes forward, I take a page and, with permission of the author, I perform it. Others usually follow suit. Once they catch on to the procedure, reading just what they have written, the students seem to find their individual rhythms. The repetitions, splices, spacings, the sounds of the vowels and consonants, the variations in pace

—*Ria Theresa*

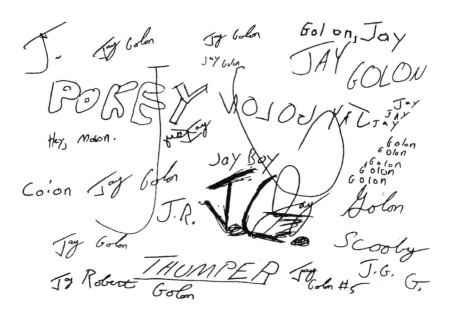

—*Jay Golon*

—*Jessica Rotondi*

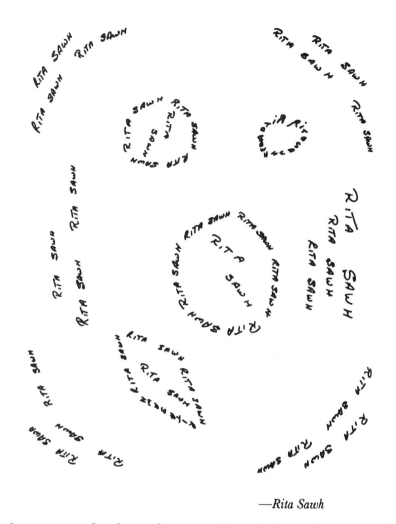

—*Rita Sawh*

and tone are perfect for performance. Everybody can hear that this is a "music"—another source of poetry.

Our best efforts at the teaching of writing enable students to experience themselves as makers of something new. They find the pleasure of investigating words and manipulating their visual patterns and sounds—thus playing with meaning. Once they do this, they are more ready to make poems. After seeing what can be made out of names, they are willing to focus on language—to arrange and shape favorite words, natural speech, or any word pool we help them find. They learn about "loving the name of anything" (Gertrude Stein's definition of poetry). They are also better able to see and hear the poem on the page, to break conventions, to invent, to make music.

Christian McEwen

Mrs. Rainey's Grandma

LIKE MOST WRITERS, I make my living doing other things. Mostly, I teach. For the last two or three years I have been teaching oral history in the New York City public schools, asking kids to start collecting family stories. The exercise that follows works best with children between the ages of eight and thirteen, though it could certainly be adapted to other groups.

On the very first day, before I mention "listening skills" and "closed and open questions" or any other jargon of the trade, I talk to the children about what I call the "silent interview." Standing at the board, I ask them one question: "What do you know about me without even asking?" "You're a girl," someone says. "A woman." "Yes, and what else?" "You're old." "All right. How old do you think?" "I dunno. Twenty-nine. Forty-two." All ages merge into one beyond the giant barrier of puberty. "What else?" "You wear nice earrings." "What else?" "You come from England, maybe. Ireland? Australia?"

They also guess at my weight, my height, the color of my hair. (Is it brown? dark brown? black? What *is* the word?) Unless pushed, they will not mention race. They will not say, "You are white," not even if I have a black woman standing right beside me, and they are interviewing us both—race is such a charged issue that they avoid it altogether. So I have to spell it out. "It is not an insult to tell me I am white, or to tell my friend here she is black. You think we don't know? You think we never looked in the mirror?" This gets some awkward laughter. But I can tell they're relieved when we move on to something else.

I use myself as subject for this first "silent interview," and for good reason. I need to get a sense of the class (shy, bold, imaginative, outrageous, etc.), and it helps to have the chance to troubleshoot a little. I also want to take advantage of the children's natural curiosity. After all, I am a stranger—they don't know anything about me. But their teacher—their regular classroom teacher—is in an altogether different position. She has a public face to maintain. She has to work with these same kids day after day, week after week. She may not want them to know too much about her. Can I teach her students to conduct an oral history interview, with her as subject, and at the same time preserve her privacy? Just as importantly, can I do this so she enjoys herself, so that she becomes (however briefly) a star in her own classroom? This exercise, "Mrs. Rainey's Grandma," is my answer to these questions.

Let's imagine that I've been asked to teach a short-term oral history workshop in a Manhattan elementary school. I've introduced myself to the teacher, whose name is Mrs. Rainey, and I like her immediately. She admits that her class is a little wild at times (they're a mixed group of fifth and sixth graders, about twenty-five in all), but she doesn't let that bother her. I get the sense that she doesn't let anything bother her very much. She's a sturdy woman, in her mid-forties, warm, wry, and level-headed, with a definite twinkle in her eye. She's ideal for what I have in mind.

It is Monday afternoon, right after school, and my oral history workshop has been scheduled for the following Thursday. Its title is something like "Roots & Branches: My Family Tree." "How would you feel," I ask Mrs. Rainey, "if the children were to interview you?"

"Me?" She looks surprised. "I thought this thing was supposed to be about the children's grandparents."

"Well, yes," I say. "Ideally, yes. But as you said, a lot of the kids in your class are recent immigrants. God knows where their grandparents are—Guatemala, Puerto Rico. . . ."

"Russia, Korea, Vietnam." She sighs. "So what are you suggesting?"

I am suggesting that the children interview Mrs. Rainey not as herself, but in the *character of her grandmother.*

"My grandmother?" she says. "You want me to play-act my own grandmother?" She laughs aloud. "You know, that's not such a bad idea. My mother's mother used to live with us. Granny O'Donnell. I spent a lot of time with her when I was a child."

"So it shouldn't be too difficult," I say, encouragingly.

"Not at all." She smiles, and jots down a note at the back of her assignment book. "Granny O'D. Thurs. a.m."

"Okay," she says to me. "Okay."

Obviously not all teachers will take to this assignment as swiftly and easily as Mrs. Rainey. Some teachers may feel anxious and uneasy. "Do I have to answer every single question?" "No," I reassure them.

"Absolutely not. If you don't want to answer something, just say so. 'I don't want to answer that,' or, 'No comment.'" Others may worry about accuracy: "What if I can't remember something? We're talking thirty-five years ago, you know." "Make it up!" I urge them. "Invent!" Often they are a little disconcerted. "This is supposed to be oral history?" But soon they begin to relax. "It's not till Thursday, right? Okay, that gives me some time."

Most teachers are chronically overscheduled, but I suggest that they do a little homework before the interview. "Take a look at some old photographs," I say. "Talk to your brother, your sister, your great-aunt. See if you can remember the way your grandmother used to stand, the clothes she liked to wear—her favorite clothes, not her best ones. What were her friends like? What sorts of things gave her pleasure? Was she a gardener, a churchgoer, did she like to travel?"

By Thursday morning, a teacher like Mrs. Rainey is fairly glowing with her own accumulated memories. When I enter the classroom, she calls me to the back, and pulls out a faded brown photograph of her grandmother "taken in her prime," as well as two or three later ones, in color. She tells me that her grandmother's name was Delia Mary Elizabeth O'Donnell, that she was born in Galway, Ireland, in 1898, and died in Brooklyn at the age of eighty-six.

"Eighty-six," I repeat admiringly. I ask her what age she wants to be, she, Mrs. Rainey, when she takes on her grandmother's character. She decides on seventy-nine. "She still had her eyesight then. Oh, she was a sharp one! She could hear well, too, even without her hearing aid."

Part of me would like nothing better than to hunker down at the back of the room and listen to Mrs. Rainey whisper stories about her grandmother. But this is a classroom, and there is work to be done. I take one last look at the beautiful Delia O'Donnell, with her two small sons leaning into her lap, and her baby daughter (Mrs. Rainey's mother) seated on her knee, and I go up to the front of the class.

"I want to let you know that we will have a visitor today," I tell the children. "And you are going to have the chance to do an interview."

Who is the visitor? Where have I hidden her? Or perhaps it is a man. Could it be Mr. Signorelli down the hall? The school custodian? Over by the window, Charisma can hardly contain herself. "Is it you, Ms. McEwen? Oh, who is it?" At this point, I refuse to say anything. I just smile mysteriously, grin at Mrs. Rainey, and start in on the lesson.

Apart from children who have obviously been cowed in some way, who come from families where violence or drink or craziness requires them to be seen and not heard, I have seldom met a child who is not delighted at the chance to ask questions. But asking questions is one thing, thinking them out in advance is something else altogether. And as for writing them down—that can be sheer drudgery.

Still, I put my professional hat on, and I talk to the children as if they were a group of aspiring journalists. I tell them everything I already know about Delia O'Donnell—Mrs. Delia O'Donnell, I call her—remembering her age, and wanting them to be polite. I tell them that her full name is Delia Mary Elizabeth O'Donnell, and that she is seventy-nine years old. I write these things up on the board. *Delia Mary Elizabeth O'Donnell. 79.* Then I pull down the big map of the world, and explain that Mrs. O'Donnell was born in Galway, Ireland, in 1898. Does anybody know where Ireland is? Yes, Charisma's friend Pauline has some idea. She comes up to the front of the class, and first locates France, then England, then, from close up, the rugged bear-shape that is Ireland. I point out Galway over on the west coast. And then I add this information to our list: *Galway, Ireland. 1898.*

We now have four or five items up on the board, all of them relating to Mrs. O'Donnell. But there is a lot more to be discovered. I encourage the children to come up with some specific questions: what else don't we know about our visitor? I begin to reel off a possible list, and soon the kids join in. What is Mrs. O'Donnell's favorite color? How many brothers and sisters does she have? What did her father do? Her mother? Did she go to school when she was little? If so, what were her favorite subjects?

Gradually we collect a list of questions, some giddy and lighthearted, some utterly serious. Carlos in the front row wants to know if there was pizza in Ireland in 1908. Soft-voiced Mary Hwong, sitting right behind him, has figured out that Delia O'Donnell must be dead by now, and wonders if she "liked being alive."

I try not to comment, but at times I can't resist, especially when a question seems unusually subtle or original. At this point, I also take the opportunity to talk a bit about technique—such as the difference between "closed" and "open" questions. Does anyone know the difference? Charisma does. (Of course!) "A closed question is a question that only has one answer," she explains. "Like?" "Like, 'Did you play hopscotch when you were little?' And then the person answers, 'Yes' or 'No.'" "And what about an open question?" Charisma knows that too. "An open question is when the person can say lots of things. You ask, 'What *kinds* of games did you play when you were a kid?' And the person says, 'Oh, I played hopscotch and I went fishing with my brother and I liked to sew and. . . .'" Charisma runs out of breath, and Mrs. Rainey, who's been watching from the back, looks down at her attendance book and smiles.

I thank Charisma and take a few minutes to quiz the rest on follow-up questions. "If Mrs. O'Donnell says she has eight brothers and sisters, what might you want to ask her next?" This time there are so many hands waving that I know I don't have to worry any more. Clearly the class is ready to get started.

"All right," I say. "Our visitor is going to join us any moment now. Before she arrives, I want you to write down four questions— only four. They can be new questions, or they can be some of the same questions that we listed earlier. I don't mind. Just remember, please, to be polite. If you ask something that is deliberately rude or insulting, Mrs. O'Donnell won't answer you. She'll skip you and go on to the next person. Remember too, that she is seventy-nine, so be sure to speak slowly and clearly and don't interrupt each other. We really need her to hear everything we're saying."

Silence follows, and six long minutes pass, as the students write down their four questions.

Then, with as much panache as I can muster, I lead Mrs. Rainey to the front of the room, and introduce her to the class as Mrs. Delia O'Donnell. I ask for a round of applause for our visitor, and the children, somewhat startled, start to clap. I point again to the few words on the blackboard. "These are the only things we know about Mrs. O'Donnell," I tell them. "Let's see what else you can find out."

This is the moment when the kids go haywire. Their arms are flailing; they are leaning forward, desperate, suffused, each one mouthing silently, "Ask me! Call on me!" Standing at the board, taking notes, it's as much as I can do to keep up with them. They want to know everything they can about Mrs. O'Donnell's childhood; about her father, Patrick Martin, who ran a stationery store; about her mother, Betsy Rose; about her brother Joseph, who was a fisherman. Carlos discovers that no, there was no pizza in Ireland in 1908, but instead there were potato pancakes, which are just as good. He learns that Mrs. O'Donnell's favorite color is green, "that deep blue-green, like the sea." Mary Hwong writes these things down in her notebook. Then Charisma asks what school was like when Mrs. O'Donnell was a little girl, and when she got married (if she did), and how many children she has (if she had any). Mrs. O'Donnell answers that she always loved school, because it was warm in the winter—"There was a lovely peat fire"—and that her husband's name was David (John David O'Donnell). He died of cancer, she says, in 1953. Then she shows everyone a tiny, framed photograph of her husband as a young man, and the big studio portrait of herself and her three children. She tells them that if she had her life to do over again, she would do it just the same, even though she suffers terribly with arthritis, especially in her left arm, and she grew up the hard way, really she did, and didn't get to fly in an airplane till she was nearly sixty-two.

I stand back a moment, watching. The questions fill the air. Carlos and Pauline, and Jose over by the door, and then Carlos again, and then Charisma. For a moment I feel anxious about the intensity of the interrogation. Can our visitor hear all right? Will she be overwhelmed? But Mrs. O'Donnell takes it all in her stride. In fact, she seems to share several very useful attributes with her granddaughter, Mrs. Rainey. At one point, when things have gotten exceptionally loud, she leans forward in her chair and cups her ears. "Holy Mother of God, I can't hear a word that child is saying. Would you repeat that now, Jose?" (To which Jose, always quick off the mark, responds, "Aw, Mrs. O'Donnell, who told you my name?")

Meanwhile some of the slower, more phlegmatic kids are baffled. "But that's Mrs. Rainey!" "Yes," I tell them, "but today she is pretending to be her grandmother." I don't beat about the bush. We have serious business to do today. We go on with the interview.

About now, Charisma, Carlos, and the other, quicker kids begin to figure out that this "Mrs. O'Donnell" is a pipeline to priceless information about Mrs. Rainey. "Have you ever met our teacher, Mrs. Rainey? Oh, she's your granddaughter! Is she your favorite? What year was *she* born? What was *she* like as a child? Was she ever *really bad?*" (I had one class where the kids wanted *more than anything in the world* to discover their teacher's middle name, and contorted every question to try to elicit it.) "Mrs. O'Donnell doesn't have to answer *everything* you ask her," I remind the children. "Please remember that she is an old lady, and that her memory isn't always so good any more." The teacher can also take the lead in this. Some will err on the side of caution. Others, like Mrs. Rainey, will do their best to answer everything. The kids appreciate such honesty enormously. (I will always remember the teacher who answered "Not exactly," when the children asked her if her grandmother was married. It was a wonderful moment, and I think was terrifically reassuring to the kids, many of whom came from single-parent families.)

Meanwhile, in Mrs. Rainey's class, the interview draws to a close. But for as long as it lasts, I continue to write crucial details on the board. I don't write complete sentences, just a simple list, so the information is up there on the board for the kids to see, and the spelling is available if it is needed.

Finally, when most of the students in the room have asked their four questions (and then some!), I thank Mrs. O'Donnell, shake her hand, and make a big fanfare of bidding her farewell: "Thank you *so* much for visiting our classroom, Mrs. O'Donnell. We *really* enjoyed having you. Okay kids, let's have another round of applause for our visitor!"

And the children do applaud, because, after all, they have enjoyed themselves, and Mrs. O'Donnell is a nice lady, even if she does bear a remarkable resemblance to her granddaughter, Mrs. Rainey (who now gets up and returns to her seat at the back of the room).

At this point there are probably ten to fifteen minutes left in the class period (if we are lucky, and I've been able to schedule a complete hour). This time is precious. Before the excitement has died down and all the lively moments dwindle to a dead list of names and phrases on the blackboard, I try to ride the last crest of the last wave—to get the children to write something down about Mrs. O'Donnell. I don't make it too difficult. I don't ask them to provide specific answers to specific questions. I tell them they can write anything at all, anything they remember. They can write about the stories her mother told at night, in the little kitchen behind the stationery store. They can write about the journey to America and how frightening it was, and the young woman Mrs. O'Donnell met on the boat, who remained her friend for life. They can write about her three children, and her eight grandchildren, and the wild one with the dark brown eyes, whose name is Elizabeth Rainey. It doesn't matter. The important thing is to write *something*. After all, I tell them, they are journalists, and there is no question that real journalists have to write—they don't just talk to the President and then go home and play video games. I also insinuate that this interview with Mrs. O'Donnell, brief though it was, might just turn out to be the first step in a long career in the media. You never can tell.

So once again, there is a brief six or eight minutes of silence while everyone writes down what he or she remembers. After that, three or four people read aloud. Mary Hwong (who seems to have retained *everything*); Carlos; Charisma; Jose, of course; Pauline. And then the class is over. With luck, it will be the first in a long series of "Roots & Branches" days in which the children interview their parents and grandparents, and then, essentially, write a little book about them, perhaps illustrating it with maps or family trees or Xeroxed photographs, perhaps branching out into "memory boxes"* or large-scale portraits. Ideally, the whole school becomes part of the collaboration, as the history teacher (who is already teaching the kids about Ellis Island) starts to think about other, more recent immigrants right there in the back row, and the art teacher (whose class is across the hall from Mrs. Rainey's) finds herself inspired to create a vast cardboard tree on which smaller, individual family trees are then displayed. Anything is possible—as I always tell the kids—and that, of course, is why I asked Mrs. Rainey's grandma to come to school in the first place.

---

* Memory boxes are modelled on the boxes made by artist Joseph Cornell. In the classrooms I was in, the children usually used shoe boxes, which they decorated with anything that took their fancy: bottle tops, plastic jewelry, crayons, poster paint, photocopies of precious family photographs. The idea was to make a kind of zany shrine to a particular person, using the colors or textures or images that that person would enjoy.

OPAL PALMER ADISA, Jamaican born, is a literary critic, writer, storyteller, and Associate Professor at California College of the Arts and Crafts. Her books include *Tamarind and Mango Women* (Sister Vision Press), *traveling women* (Jukebox Press), *Bake-Face and Other Guava Stories* (Kelsey Street Press), and *Pina, the Many-Eyed Fruit* (Julian Richards & Associates).

JACK COLLOM is the author of many books of poetry and two books on teaching writing: *Moving Windows* (T&W) and, with Sheryl Noethe, *Poetry Everywhere* (T&W). He is the recipient of two poetry fellowships from the National Endowment for the Arts. Collom lives in Boulder, Colorado.

MARGOT FORTUNATO GALT is a poet who has taught imaginative writing at all levels. She received a Ph.D. in American Studies from the University of Minnesota. In 1992, T&W published her book *The Story in History: Writing Your Way into the American Experience.*

CYNDE GREGORY has worked as a poet in the schools since 1975. Her books include *Childmade: Awakening Children to Creative Writing* (Station Hill) and *Quick and Easy Learning Centers: Writing* (Scholastic). For two years she served as columnist for *Instructor* magazine.

GEOFF HEWITT is the author of *A Portfolio Primer: Teaching, Collecting, and Assessing Student Writing* (Heinemann). Hewitt, the Writing/Secondary English Consultant for the Vermont State Department of Education, visits schools across the country to lead writing workshops for students and teachers. In 1989 Ithaca House published his second book of poems, *Just Worlds.*

ROLAINE HOCHSTEIN's short stories have been published widely. Her novels are *Stepping Out* (Norton) and *Table 47* (Doubleday). Her nonfiction books, written with Daniel A. Sugarman, Ph.D., are *The Seventeen Guide to Knowing Yourself* and *The Seventeen Guide to You and Other People* (Macmillan). She works as a writer in the schools for the New Jersey State Council on the Arts.

LIZA KETCHUM teaches writing to students of all ages, and has been an adjunct faculty member at Emerson College, Antioch, New England Graduate School, and Lesley College. Under the name Liza

Ketchum Murrow, she has published nine books for children and young adults, including *Twelve Days in August* (Holiday House). Ketchum lives in Clinton, Massachusetts.

JANICE LOWE is a poet, composer, and teacher. Her poems have appeared in *Callaloo* and *In the Tradition: An Anthology of Young Black Writers*. Her musical works have been performed at La Mama E.T.C., the Nuyorican Poets Cafe, and NADA Theatre. Co-founder of the Dark Room Collective, she coaches poetry writing workshops for children throughout New York City.

CHRISTIAN MCEWEN has taught in the New York City public schools and at the Parsons School of Design. She is the editor of two anthologies of lesbian writers, as well as the forthcoming collection *Tomboys* (Beacon). A founding member of the intergenerational theater group, Roots & Branches, McEwen lives in the hills of western Massachusetts.

DAVID MILLS received an M.A. in Poetry from New York University. He has taught poetry writing and playwriting in the schools and prisons since 1990. In 1993 he received the BRIO award for poetry. His writing has appeared in *Downbeat, The Village Voice, Essence,* and other periodicals. His play *The Serpent and the Dove* was produced by the Juillard School of Drama.

ELIZABETH RABY is a poet who teaches writing at all levels. Her books include *The Hard Scent of Peonies* (Jasper Press) and *Camphorwood* (Nightshade Press). She has worked in the New Jersey and Pennslyvania state writers-in-the-schools programs, and teaches poetry writing for the Geraldine R. Dodge Foundation. She holds an M.A. in Creative Writing from Temple University.

ROSANNE M. ROPPEL has taught English in Idaho and Alaska since 1975. Chairperson of the Alaska State Writing Consortium Board, she was also a member of the Alaska 2000 Review Committee, restructuring the Alaskan language arts curriculum. A Dewitt Wallace Rural Network fellowship has enabled her to spend summers studying at the Bread Loaf School of English.

MARK STATMAN has taught for Teachers & Writers Collaborative and at Eugene Lang College at the New School for Social Research since 1984. His writing has appeared in *Transfer, Notus, Democracy & Educa-*

tion, The Nation, and *The Village Voice.* Statman has received fellowships from the National Endowment for the Arts and the National Writers Project.

SAM SWOPE has taught writing in New York City public schools since 1989. A frequent reviewer of children's books, he is the author of two: *The Araboolies of Liberty Street* (Clarkson Potter) and *The Krazees* (Farrar Straus & Giroux). He helped edit *Saving Wildlife* (Abrams), an anthology from the New York Zoological Society.

MADELINE TIGER has worked as a writer in the schools for the New Jersey State Council on the Arts for more than twenty years. She also teaches in the Geraldine R. Dodge Foundation program. Her recent books of poems include *My Father's Harmonica* (Nightshade Press) and *Mary of Migdal* (Still Waters Press). One of her essays on teaching appeared in *Educating the Imagination* (T&W).

MARK GRANT WAREN is a playwright and theater artist whose work has been performed in theaters and festivals around the U.S. New York productions include *Mexico* (at the Bouwerie Lane Theatre) and *Lust and the Unicorn* (at La Mama E.T.C.). Waren teaches writing in the T&W program.

MEREDITH SUE WILLIS is a fiction writer who has taught writing at all levels. Three of her novels were published by Scribner's. Her recent fiction includes a collection of stories, *In the Mountains of America* (Mercury House), and a children's novel, *The Secret Super Powers of Marco* (HarperCollins). T&W has published her three books on teaching writing: *Personal Fiction Writing, Blazing Pencils,* and *Deep Revision.*

DALE WORSLEY is the author of a novel, *The Focus Changes of August Previco;* a novella, *Hoy;* the plays *Cold Harbor, Blue Devils,* and *The Last Living Newspaper;* and numerous essays on teaching writing. He received National Endowment for the Arts fellowships in fiction and playwriting and EDPRESS awards for his essays. T&W published *The Art of Science Writing,* which he co-authored with Bernadette Mayer.

OTHER T&W PUBLICATIONS YOU MIGHT ENJOY

The Teachers & Writers Handbook of Poetic Forms, edited by Ron Padgett. This T&W bestseller includes 74 entries on traditional and modern poetic forms by 19 poet-teachers. "A treasure"—*Kliatt*. "The definitions not only inform, they often provoke and inspire. A small wonder!"—*Poetry Project Newsletter*. "An entertaining reference work"—*Teaching English in the Two-Year College*. "A solid beginning reference source"—*Choice*.

Personal Fiction Writing by Meredith Sue Willis. A complete and practical guide for teachers of writing from elementary through college level. Contains more than 340 writing ideas. "A terrific resource for the classroom teacher as well as the novice writer"—*Harvard Educational Review*.

Educating the Imagination, Vols. 1 & 2, edited by Christopher Edgar and Ron Padgett. A big selection of the best articles from 17 years of *Teachers & Writers* magazine, with ideas and assignments for writing poetry, fiction, plays, history, folklore, parodies, and much more.

The Story in History: Writing Your Way into the American Experience by Margot Fortunato Galt. Combines imaginative writing and American history. "One of the best idea books for teachers I have ever read"—*Kliatt*.

The List Poem: A Guide to Teaching & Writing Catalog Verse by Larry Fagin defines list poetry, traces its history, gives advice on teaching it, offers specific writing ideas, and presents more than 200 examples by children and adults. An *Instructor* Poetry Pick. "Outstanding"—*Kliatt*.

Poetry Everywhere: Teaching Poetry Writing in School and in the Community by Jack Collom & Sheryl Noethe. This big and "tremendously valuable resource work for teachers" (*Kliatt*) at all levels contains 60 writing exercises, extensive commentary, and 450 example poems.

The Writing Workshop, Vols. 1 & 2 by Alan Ziegler. A perfect combination of theory, practice, and specific assignments. "Invaluable to the writing teacher"—*Contemporary Education*. "Indispensable"—Herbert R. Kohl.

The Whole Word Catalogue, Vols. 1 & 2. T&W's bestselling guides to teaching imaginative writing. "*WWC 1* is probably the best practical guide for teachers who really want to stimulate their students to write"—*Learning*. "*WWC 2* is excellent. . . . It makes available approaches to the teaching of writing not found in other programs"—*Language Arts*.

❖

For a complete free catalogue of T&W books, magazines, audiotapes, videotapes, and computer writing games, contact
Teachers & Writers Collaborative,
5 Union Square West, New York, NY 10003–3306,
(212) 691-6590.